The Collectors Encyclopedia of

IESTA

With Harlequin and Riviera

by
Sharon & Bob Huxford

COLLECTOR BOOKS
A Division of Schroeder Publishing Co., Inc.

P.O. BOX 3009   PADUCAH, KENTUCKY   42001

Additional copies of this book may be ordered from:

COLLECTOR BOOKS
P.O. Box 3009
Paducah, Kentucky   42001
or
The authors: Sharon & Bob Huxford
1202 7th Street
Covington, Indiana   47932

$8.95 plus 50¢ for postage

Printed by Taylor Publishing Company, Dallas, Texas

With deepest appreciation
this book
is dedicated to

Leslie and Marjorie Wolfe,

our friends
and collaborators

TABLE OF CONTENTS

FOREWORD

Lest there be those who are still unaware . . . "Fiesta has arrived"!! In bright, cheery, colorful capital letters!!! Gone are the days when we checked under the tables in the "junk" boxes at the flea markets . . . scoured mall shows with little or no avail . . . and antique shops! Don't you remember retorting (just a little defensively) "We just want to look around", in order to avoid one of those slightly distainful sidelong glances we knew so well — and yet hoping all the while to find one nice piece dejectedly occupying some dark, forgotten corner.

We've come a long way, Baby! Out of those dark ages, into the "Fiesta Generation"! Can you believe that now there are whole tables of Fiesta at those same flea markets!!! . . . beautifully colorful booths at the mall shows displaying nothing *but* Fiesta, Harlequin and Riviera! But don't dismay if you still find no Fiesta in that little antique shop, for more than likely, the owner is collecting it herself!

And the numbers of collectors are continuing to grow, judging from your letters (and our book sales) . . . we've recently noticed a spurt of interest in Ontario, Canada — who knows how far-reaching "Fiesta Fever" may become??

From your letters, new facts and information have reached us which we want to share with all of you. And again, it has become necessary to offer a revised price guide in order to keep you abreast of current market values. We consider it a pleasure to offer this, our third edition . . . we hope you will enjoy it.

ACKNOWLEDGEMENTS

May we say first of all, that we are grateful to each one of you, our readers, for your interest, your enthusiasm, your most appreciated support. Of the thousands of names on our mailing list, some have become quite familiar to us, though we've never personally met. We thank every one of you, who through your letters have shared your ideas and discoveries with us.

Special thanks go to these people who have specifically contributed to this edition. Some actually packed up their treasures and sent them to us . . . and others helped in various ways:

Austin and Lucille Wilson	Muriel Feldt
Betty Brewster	Nancy and Willie Dillahunt
Paula Ashby	Martie and Bill Higgins
Linda and Jim Lewis	Geraldine Deputy
Kenton Kirsting	Mike Printz
Hazel Hazen	Susan Graves
Dick and Diane Knowles	Sandi Maston
Tom and Phyllis Bess	Jerry and Linda Kukla
Helen McKenzie	Betty Frisbie

John Sanders

More than words can express, we do so very much appreciate the help and information supplied by Mr. Ed Carson, representative of the Homer Laughlin China Company. We've plied him with questions for years now, and he continues to be always generous and gracious to us. As this field continues to grow, further research becomes more detailed and difficult to obtain, and aside from knowledge gained from veteran collectors, factory records are our only source of official information.

In three editions, we've had that many photographers, each one superior. Donahue Studios of Evansville, Ind. did the first edition pictures, Dana Curtis of Paducah, Ky. the second, and Dowers Studios of Danville, Ill., the third. This edition contains some of the work of all three.

Once again, we've dedicated our book to Leslie and Marjorie Wolfe. They've opened their home to us many times, and we've discussed new finds, colors, and price trends for hours on end, more often than not over a delicious dinner! Words simply cannot properly convey our thanks for the tremendous help they've been to us, and for their friendship.

Thank you all . . . and may God Bless . . .

ABOUT THE AUTHORS

From a long-time interest in collecting, the Huxfords have expanded their hobby to include research and writing, and both agree they find this field to be most exciting and rewarding. Their first book, *The Story of Fiesta* was published in 1974, followed two years later with a revised second edition, *The Collectors Encyclopedia of Fiesta.* They have written several other books dealing with the Ohio potteries . . . *The Collectors Encyclopedia of Roseville Pottery* and *The Collectors Catalogue of Early Roseville* were published in 1976; new releases in 1978 include *The Collectors Encyclopedia of McCoy Pottery, The Collectors Encyclopedia of Brush-McCoy Pottery,* and *The Collectors Catalogue of Brush-McCoy Pottery.* They have written articles for both *The Glaze* and *The Depression Glass Daze,* and have been named Pottery Editors for Collector Books.

THE LAUGHLIN POTTERY STORY

The Laughlin Pottery was formed in 1871 on the River Road in East Liverpool, Ohio — the result of a partnership between Homer Laughlin and his brother, Shakespear Laughlin. The pottery was equipped with two periodic kilns and was among the first in the country to produce whitewares. Sixty employees produced approximately 500 dozen pieces of dinnerware per day. The superior quality of their pottery won for them the highest award at the Centennial Exposition in Philadelphia in 1876.

In 1879, Shakespear Laughlin left the pottery, and, for the next 10 years, Homer Laughlin carried on the business alone. William Edwin Wells joined him in 1889 and, at the end of 1896, the firm incorporated. Shortly thereafter, Laughlin sold his interests to Wells and a Pittsburgh group headed by Marcus Aaron.

Under the new management, Mr. Aaron became President, with Mr. Wells acting in the capacity of Secretary-Treasurer and General Manager.

As their business grew and sales increased, the small River Road plant was abandoned and the company moved its location to Laughlin Station, three miles east of East Liverpool. Two large new plants were constructed and a third purchased from another company. By 1903, all were ready for production. A fourth plant was built in 1906 at the Newell, West Virginia site, and began operation in 1907. In 1913, with business still increasing, Plant 5 was added.

The first revolutionary innovation in the pottery industry was the continuous tunnel kiln. In contrast to the old batch-type, or periodic kilns which were inefficient from a standpoint of both fuel and time, the continuous tunnel kiln provided a giant step toward modern day mass production. Plant 6, built in 1923, was equipped with this new type kiln and proved so successful that two more such

8

plants were added, Plant 7, in 1927, and Plant 8, in 1929. The old kilns in Plants 4 and 5 were replaced in 1926 and 1934 respectively.

In 1929 the old East Liverpool factories were closed, leaving the entire operation at the Newell, West Virginia site.

At the height of their production the company grew to a giant concern which employed 2,500 people, produced thirty thousand dozen pieces of dinnerware per day, and utilized 1,500,000 square feet of production area. In contrast to the early wares, painstakingly hand-fashioned in the traditional methods, the style of ware reflected the improved mass production techniques which had of necessity been utilized in later years. The old-fashioned dipping tubs gave way to the use of high-speed conveyor belts and spray glazing, and mechanical jiggering machines replaced for the most part the older methods of man powered molding machines.

In 1930, W. E. Wells retired from the business after more than 40 years of brilliant leadership, having guided the development and expansion of the company from its humble beginning on the Ohio river to a position of unquestioned leadership in its field. He was succeeded by his son, Joseph Mahan Wells. Mr. Aaron became Chairman of the Board, and his son, M. L. Aaron, succeeded him as President. Under their leadership, in addition to the successful wares already in production, many new developments made possible the production of a wide variety of utilitarian wares including the oven-to-table ware, Oven Serve and Kitchen Kraft. Later, the creation of the beautiful colored glazes which have become almost synonymous with Homer Laughlin, resulted in the production of the colored dinnerware lines which have captured the attention of many collectors today — Fiesta, Harlequin, and Riviera.

On January 1, 1960, Joseph M. Wells became Chairman of the Board, and his son Joseph M. Wells, Jr. followed him in the capacity of Executive Vice-President.

Today, Homer Laughlin employs 1,600 workers, producing approximately 60 million pieces of dinnerware per year.

VACATIONING IN THE MORGUE???
(we loved it!)

Have you ever awakened from your dreams, been able to close your eyes once again, concentrate very hard, and remember some heretofore completely unheard of piece of Fiesta . . . or Harlequin . . . or Riviera? I remember some fantastic tall stemmed mugs that distinctly and to my absolute joy were marked "Genuine Fiesta" when I turned them up to check!! How disappointing to discover it was only a dream!

Last fall, on a return trip to HLC, we were allowed an experience that was to us as exciting as having our dreams come true. We were granted permission to explore the "morgue"! What a name to call such a delightful place! Better than any junk store . . . more "goodies" than anyone could dream of!

We dug in shelves and boxes to our hearts' content. We photographed and catalogued all the things we found. Jane, a very sweet lady in engineering, kept all the Fiesta we dug out and cleaned up together in boxes, in hopes that someday a display might be arranged for future visitors to enjoy.

There were familiar Fiesta, Harlequin and Riviera there, to be sure; but what captured our attention were the many experimental pieces. The very first beautiful and unfamiliar piece of Fiesta we saw was an ivory individual tea pot with a stick handle, 6" tall. It had a globular shape, and its lid was interchangeable with the demitasse coffee pot. Although it was never produced for the market, at least one has been found in a shop in Newell, West Virginia, by a very lucky collector!

We learned that the designer, Fredrick Rhead, modeled many pieces which were never marketed, due to the onset of the war scare . . . when lines already in production were cut back.

10

There was a relish plate with five compartments, arranged just like your Fiesta relish tray, but molded in one piece. It was in navy and was decorated with a band of rings . . . had the look of Fiesta, but may not have even been an HLC product. We were astounded to learn the extent at which potteries "borrowed" designs and patterns from each other . . . evidently very goodnaturedly.

Another piece we found was an ivory 6″ vase which might best be described as looking like the pouring end of two disk juice pitchers, back to back, with the ice lips removed! The body was a round upright disk, and the band of rings design was a complete circle, slightly indented into the front and back sides.

There was a yellow piece, 5″ across, flat and very shallow, with a narrow flat rim. Although most of the experimental pieces were marked with only code numbers, this one carried the familiar "Fiesta" cast-indented mark.

Stacked in a corner were several sections of a large relish designed by Rhead. Four trays with three compartments, each was styled with the intent of being used on a large oval wooden base. Although never released, one of these sections is shown on page 75.

A piece that looked very familiar to us, except for its size (it was 6½″ tall) was done in yellow, and scaled to perfection to the lines of the syrup bottom.

And the experimental colors were fantastic! There was a rich burgundy wine cream soup, and a relish tray done in the Wells Matt Glaze, which had the effect of iron rust. Plates were in dark brown with an orange splattered effect, a blue plum, a dark russet tone, a deep, deep gold, and our favorite of all — black with four chromium bands, which must have been 35 years ahead of its time.

Some familiar Kitchen Kraft items had been glazed in pastels — pink, light blue, pale yellow and mint green — and the mark stamped on the bottom of some identified the line as "Chromatics".

11

From a box in a corner, came the metal holder for the pie plate — the first we had seen. These, the metal holders for the Kitchen Kraft casseroles and the one for the oval Kitchen Kraft platter, were shipped to HLC and distributed from the factory with these pieces. However, not all were sold with holders. We also found the underplates for the casseroles. These were simply a flat plate with a rim, seemingly of a lighter weight than usual. We wondered if perhaps they were from another line and simply dipped in the Fiesta Kitchen Kraft colors.

Several small nut dishes with a basketweave design were stacked on a shelf, next to a larger one . . . identical except for the addition of some flowers inside the bowl. We learned that the smaller version was from the Harlequin line, and had been copied from the larger, which was a Japanese import. There was a matching bowl (but this had been only experimental, and had not been marketed), and an ash tray with the basketweave design; it also belonged to the Harlequin line.

There were two styles of experimental candlesticks in Harlequin. One pair was large and flat, 5½″ wide and 2¼″ tall in the center. The other pair were shaped like half of an inverted cone, 4¼″ across the bottom and 3″ tall. Both styles were lovely, but not quite as nice as our regular candleholders. The only other unusual Harlequin piece was a 5″ fruit, shaped almost like the small Fiesta fruit dish. There were some novel experimental colors . . . chocolate brown, deep golden tan, a pale bisque beige, lavender, vanilla, and a beautiful plate, cup and saucer in a high gloss black!

We found three sizes in Riviera butters, 9″, 6½″, and 7½″. The latter, although just the right size for a quarter-lb. stick of today's butter, was never marketed. Also strictly experimental — and what a shame — was a large footed console bowl, 15″ × 8½″ and a pair of tall, 6″ candleholders. These really were beautiful. Of all the discoveries we made, they held the most appeal to us!

Have you ever wondered about the six sections around the Riviera shakers? They were originally designed to go with the Tango line, but as the shape was compatible, they were also used with Riviera. Tango was a colored dinnerware line made for promotion through Newberry's. Colors were green, yellow, burgundy, and blue; there may have been others. The gauge was similar to Harlequin, the design was a classic Colonial style; but, for some reason, it was not a good seller.

We so thoroughly enjoyed our day in the morgue, and we felt that we would like to share some of its contents with all our readers. Although most of the beautiful pieces we saw will never be available to the collector, like the little individual tea pot, there may be a few that somehow found their way to the outside. When our day was over, we felt reluctant to close that door, with its double lock, and to have to leave behind it those lovely pieces. They were truly "stuff that dreams are made of"!

. . . that RADIOACTIVE RED!

Exactly when the first rumors began circulating . . . hinting that the red Fiesta could be "hazardous" to your health, is uncertain. In most probability, it was around the time that Fiesta red was reintroduced, after the war . . . and was no doubt due to the publicity given to uranium and radio-activity during the war years. Clearly another case where "a *little* learning can be a dangerous thing".

In any case, this worry must have remained to trouble the minds of some folks for several years. Even today the subject comes up occasionally and remains a little controversial, even though most folks in this troubled age of ozone worries, no-phosphates, or cyclamates, cholesterol-free diets, and constant reminders that "Cigarettes are hazardous to your health" don't really seem too upset by it any more.

The following letter appeared in the *Palm Beach Post Times,* in February, 1963. It was written "tongue-in-cheek" by a man who had evidently reached the limit of his patience. HLC sent it to us from their files; it has to be a classic. Here it is . . .

Editor:
After reading about the radioactive dishes in your paper I am greatly concerned that I may be in danger, as I had a plate with a design in burnt orange, or maybe it was lemon.
This plate was left to me by my great grandmother, and I noticed that whenever she ate anything from it her ears would light up so we all had to wear dark glasses when dining at her house.
I first became suspicious of this dish when putting out food for my dog on it I noticed the dog's nose became as red as Rudolph's and one

day a seagull fed from it and all his feathers fell off; then one night when the weather was raw I placed it at the foot of my bed and my toenails turned black.

Using it as a pot cover while cooking eel stew, the pot cracked; and reading the letters in your paper last week have concluded I am not the only person having a cracked pot in the house, so perhaps some of your other readers used a plate for a cover.

I finally threw this plate overboard at a turn in the channel, now a buoy is no longer needed there, as bubbles and steam mark this shoal.

Will you please ask your Doctor or someone if they think this plate was radioactive, and if so am I in any danger, and if so from what?

(Name Withheld)

In case the question ever arises in your presence, the following information will provide you with an intelligent answer. This data was measured at Purdue University in the Bionucleonics Department by Dr. Paul L. Ziemer, and Dr. Geraldine Deputy, who herself is an avid Fiesta collector. Here are the results of their study:

The penetrating radiation from the depleted uranium oxide used in the manufacturing of the glaze for the "red" Fiestaware was measured with a standard laboratory Geiger Counter. All measurements are tabularized in units of milliroentgens per hour (mR/hr).

ITEM	SURFACE CONTACT	4" ABOVE SURFACE	ALONG RIM
13" Chop Plate	0.8	0.35	0.1
9" Plate	0.5	1.5	0.07
Fruit Bowl	1.5	0.5	0.1
Relish Tray Wedge	0.8	0.2	0.02
Cup	1.3	0.2	0.03

In order to compare the above values to familiar quantities of radiation we calculated the exposure of a person holding a 13" chop plate strapped to his chest for 24 hours. This gives 20 milliroentgens per day. Safe levels for humans working with radiation is 100 milliroentgens per week for a 5 day week or 20 milliroentgens per day as background radiation.

Some other measurements of interest for comparison purposes are:

ITEM	RADIATION
Radium Dial on a Watch	20 mR/hr
Chest X-Ray	44mR per film
Dental X-Ray	910 mR per film
Fatal Dose	400,000 mR over whole body

So you see — unless you've noticed your grandmother's nose glowing — we're all quite safe!

One other *tiny* worry to put to rest . . . some have mentioned it . . . there is no danger from the fired-on glazes which are safe as opposed to a shellac-type color which could mix with acid from certain foods, and result in lead poisoning.

Wouldn't it be good to get back to the days when worries were simple and uncomplicated . . . and everybody cooked with lard and had never heard of cholesterol . . . and air pollution was just something to be washed off white enameled woodwork at spring cleaning time . . . and gas was 25¢ a gallon . . .

Post Script: As recently as May, 1977, on an Eastern television station, an announcement was made concerning the pros and cons of the safety of colored glazed dinnerware. Fiesta was mentioned by name. We contacted the Department of Health, Education and Welfare, FDA, in Chicago, Illinois. This in part is their position, and is supported by HLC:

> "The presence of lead, cadium and other toxic metal in glaze or decal is not in itself a hazard. It becomes a problem only when a glaze or decal that has not been properly formulated, applied or fired, contains dangerous metals which can be released by high acid foods such as fruit juices, some soft drinks, wines, cider, vinegar and vinegar containing foods, sauerkraut, and tomato products" . . .

HLC passed the rigorous federal tests with flying colors! In fact, the only examples of earthenware posing a threat to consumers were imported, and hobbyists were warned to use extreme caution in glazing hand thrown ceramics.

The FDA report continues:

"be on the safe side by not storing foods or beverages in such containers for prolonged periods of time, such as overnight. Daily use of the dinnerware for serving food *does not* pose a hazard. If the glaze or decal is properly formulated, properly applied, and properly fired, there is no hazard."

. . . R. I. P.

A WORD TO THE WISE . . .

Haven't we all had the experience of finding a likely looking piece of pottery . . . we ponder and study, turn it over and over, flip the rim to make it ring, compare color and glaze, weight and thickness . . . and still be at a complete loss???

Probably the most important lesson to be learned, especially in this area of collecting, is that no matter how good a piece looks, be extremely suspicious! Styles, designs, decorations, and even glazes were flagrantly copied from one pottery by another. Whole lines were stolen from pottery dumps!

Several pieces have been the objects of such discussion. They are similar in body, color, glaze and design; and yet they are not Fiesta, nor were they even produced by HLC. Perhaps the one most often in question is the little child's pitcher that looks so much like the Fiesta disk pitcher. If you tour many flea-markets, you most certainly have seen one of these. But HLC says they did not produce this or any other child's pieces.

On a few occasions we have been so sure of a new discovery that we were almost inclined to argue with those "in-the-know" at HLC; but they continue to caution us of the many attempts made by others to profit from the popularity of Fiesta by producing a very good imitation of their own. (There was even a copy from a Japanese company!) So be very dubious . . . all that glitters is not gold!

There may even yet be an undiscovered item or two . . . perhaps a one-of-a-kind whimsy created by an inventive craftsman. These things have always been. Even through the years of mass production, that desire innate in every living person to make something with his own hands, using his own ideas is strong in his breast. The temptation to create in an environment where all the necessary materials and equipment are available would be too much for one so inclined to put from his mind! Several times we have been told of a "Fiesta lamp". HLC tells us they did not produce one, but that some of their employees fashioned lamps for themselves from carafe bottoms. They also used some of the tall vases. Ever see one? We haven't.

Then of course, there are always "Fiesta butter-dish" stories from time to time. Here is HLC's statement:

"If you do find the butter in Fiesta, it will necessarily be a copy, because this certainly was one of the items that was never produced in this line based upon all records available and the memories of those people involved in designing, manufacturing, and shopping Fiesta over the years."

Last summer we saw a turquoise casserole that looked exactly like the Fiesta casserole, except this one had no foot. It was marked "Tricolator Products, U.S.A." It seemed logical to assume that these were no doubt manufactured at HLC for Tricolator Products. Right??? WRONG!!! This from HLC: *". . . it is unthinkable that with the popularity of Fiesta, that we would sell Fiesta items under another company's name."* Another imitation!

There are bulb-type candleholders very similar to Fiesta's. Salt and pepper shakers of many types — one curious set consisted of what appeared to be a genuine Fiesta salt shaker perched atop a little raised platform with a handle, which was actually the pepper! (HLC had never heard of it!)

One last item that may be confusing some of you . . . it certainly did us . . . is the pie plate with an exact duplication of the Harlequin rings. We have seen one in green, and the color is a perfect match. This is a classic example. HLC says it is not Harlequin, nor did they ever produce it. So be very cautious . . . we would welcome your inquiries in cases like these. If there are new discoveries — and there may well be — we will do our best to keep our fellow collectors informed and up to date!

THE STORY OF FIESTA

In January of 1936, Homer Laughlin introduced a sensational new line of dinnerware at the Pottery and Glass Show in Pittsburgh. It was "Fiesta" . . . and it instantly captured the imagination of the trade — a forecast of the success it was to achieve with housewives of America.

Fiesta was designed by Fredrick Rhead, an English Stoke-on-Trent potter, who was employed under the direction of M. L. Aaron, President, and J. M. Wells, Secretary and General Manager. His design was modeled by Arthur Kraft and Bill Bersford. The distinctive glazes were developed by Dr. A. V. Blenininger in association with H. W. Thiemecke.

A talc body was introduced for the first time, making Fiesta entirely different in body materials and glazes. This made it necessary to confine its production to the Number 4 plant, in Newell, West Virginia. This plant soon led all others in output and production, due to Fiesta's unprecedented popularity. Opinion in the beginning was that certain sections of the country would not like the colorful ware and the unusual shapes. However, sales were ever-increasing on a nationwide basis!

This popularity was the result of much planning, market analysis, creative development, and a fundamentally sound and well-organized styling program. Rather than present to the everyday housewife a modernistic interpretation of a formal table service which might have been received with some reservation, HLC offered a more casual line with a well-planned series of accessories whose style was compatible with any decor and whose vivid colors could add bright spots of emphasis. Services of all types could be chosen and assembled at the whim of the housewife, and the simple style could be used compatibly with other wares already in her cabinets.

In an article by Fredrick Rhead, taken from the "Crockery and

Glass Journal" for June, 1937, these steps toward Fiesta's development were noted:

First, from oral descriptions and data concerning most generally used table articles, a chart of tentative sketches in various appealing colors was made. As the final ideas were formulated, they were modified and adjusted until development was completed.

Secondly, the technical department made an intensive study of materials, compositions, and firing temperatures. During this time models and shapes were being studied. The result was to be a streamline shape, but not so obvious as to detract from the texture and color of the ware. It was to have no relief ornamentation, and was to be pleasantly curving and convex, rather than concave or angular. Color was to be the chief decorative note, but to avoid being too severe, the concentric band of rings were to be added at the edges.

Since the early thirties, there had been a very definite trend in merchandising toward promoting "color". Automobiles, household appliances and furnishings, ladies' apparel . . . all took on vivid hues. The following is an excerpt from Rhead's article: (although he relates the ivory glaze being chosen as the fifth color, it was not an original color, but was added later on in 1936).

> *"The final selection of five colors was a more difficult job because we had developed hundreds of tone values and hues and there were scores which were difficult to reject. Then, there were textures ranging from dull mattes to highly reflecting surfaces. We tackled the texture problem first. (Incidentally, we had made fair sized skeletons in each of the desirable glazes in order to be better able to arrive at the final selection.)*
>
> *We eliminated the dull mattes and the more highly reflecting glazes. First, because in mass production practice, undue variation would result in unpleasant effects. The*

dull surfaces are not easy to clean and the too highly reflecting surfaces show "curtains" or variations in thickness of application. We decided upon a semi-reflecting surface of about the texture of a billiard ball. The surface was soft and pleasant to the touch and in average light there were no disturbing reflections to detract from the color and shape.

We had one lead with regard to color. There seemed to be a trade preference for a brilliant orange red. With this color as a key note and with the knowledge that we were to have five colors, the problem resolved to one where the remainder would "tune in" or form appropriate contrasts.

The obvious reaction to red, we thought, would be toward a fairly deep blue. We had blues ranging from pale turquoises to deep violet blues. The tests were made by arranging a table for four people and, as the plate is an important item in the set, we placed four plates on various colored cloths and then arranged the different blues around the table. It seemed that the deeper blues reacted better than the lighter tones and also blues which were slightly violet or purple. We also found that we had to do considerable switching before we could decide upon the right red. Some were too harsh and deep, others too yellow.

With the red and blue apparently settled, we decided that a green must be one of the five colors. We speedily discovered that the correct balance between the blue and the red was a green possessing a minimum of blue. We had to hit halfway between the red and the blue. We had some lovely subtle greens when they were not placed in juxtaposition with the other two colors, but they would not play in combination.

The next obvious color was yellow and this had to be toned halfway between the red and the green. Only the most brilliant yellow we could make would talk in company with the other three.

The fifth color was the hardest nut to crack. Black was too heavy, although this may have been used if we could have had six or more colors. We had no browns, purples or grays which would tune in. We eliminated all except two colors: a rich turquoise and a lovely color we called rose ebony. But there seemed too much color when any fifth was introduced in any table arrangement. The quartette seemed to demand a quieting influence, so we tried an ivory vellum textured glaze which seemed to fit halfway between the yellow and the regular semi-vitreous wares and which cliqued when placed against any one of the four colors selected. It took a little time to sell the ivory to our sales organization, but when they saw the table arrangements they accepted the idea."

In the same publication, a month earlier, Rhead had offered this evaluation of the popularity of the various colors with the public:

"When this ware first appeared on the market, we attempted to estimate the preference for one color in comparison with the others. As you know, we make five colors . . . Because the red was the most expensive color, we thought this might affect the demand. And also, because green had previously been a most popular color, some guessed that this would outsell the others. However, to date, the first four colors are running neck and neck with less than one percent difference between them. This is a remarkable result and amply bears out . . . that the "layman" prefers to mix his colors."

The original assortment presented in the four colors — green, blue, yellow, and red, consisted of 54 items:

Flower vase, 10"; Coffee pot, regular; Tea pot, large; Tea Pot, medium; Coffee pot, A.D.; Carafe; Ice Pitcher; Jug, 2 pints; Covered sugar; Creamer; Bud vase; Chop plate, 15″; Chop plate, 13″; Compartment plate, 10½″; Plate, 10″; Plate, 9″; Plate, 7″; Plate, 6″; Tea cups and saucers; Coffee cups and saucers, A.D.; Footed salad bowl; Nested bowls, 11½″ to 5″; Covered casserole; Cream soup cup; Covered onion soup; Relish tray; Comport, 12″; Nappy, 9½″; Nappy, 8½″; Deep plate, 8″; Dessert, 6″; Fruit, 5″; Ash tray; Sweets comport; Candleholders, tripod; Candleholders, bulb type; Salt and pepper shakers; Marmalade; Mustard; Egg cups; Tumbler; Tom & Jerry mugs; Utility tray.

Adding further to the selling possibilities of Fiesta, in June, 1936, the company offered their "Harmony" dinnerware sets. These combined their Nautalis line decorated with a colorful decal pattern, accented and augmented with the Fiesta color selected for that particular set. N-258 featured yellow Fiesta, accenting Nautalis in white decorated with a harmonizing floral decal at the rim. N-259 used green Fiesta to complement a slender spray of pine cones. Red Fiesta, in N-260, was shown together with the Nautalis decorated with lines and leaves in an Art Deco flavor; and Blue (N-261) went well with the white Nautalis with an off-center flower-filled basket decal. These sets were composed of 76 pieces in this combination:

NAUTALIS SHAPE		FIESTA	
8	7″ plates	8	10″ plates
8	4″ plates	8	7″ plates
8	tea cups and saucers	8	6″ plates
8	4″ fruits	1	15″ chop plate
1	10″ baker	1	12″ comport
1	7″ nappy	2	bulb candlesticks
		1	salt and pepper
		1	sugar and creamer

Retail price for such a set was around $20.00; with Fiesta red increasing the total cost by about $3.50. This offered a complete service for 8 and extra pieces that allowed for buffet and party service for as many more of the contrasting items.

As Fiesta's popularity continued to bring profits to retailers, many other concerns began to attempt to capitalize on its success. Metal works companies turned out various accessories to market with the colorful ware. Retail outlets sold sets of Fiesta to which they had added plastic handled flatware in complementary colors, glass tumblers in a variety of styles, and many other items. However, none were ever produced by HLC, nor were such sets assembled by them.

Certainly one of the most elaborate sets we are aware of is today still intact and in the hands of a very happy collector. Since it contains only the original four colors, we assume it was sold early in production. There are 114 pieces, only 40 of which are Fiesta. The remainder are accessories. It contains:
    8 9" plates
    8 6" plates
    8 tea cups and saucers
    8 5" fruits
Accessories include:
    24 pc. glassware set, with Mexican decal, 8 each 10 oz., 8 oz., and 6 oz. tumblers
    8 color coordinated swizzle sticks
    8 glass ashtrays
    Service for 8, flatware with color coordinated plastic handles
    1 serving bowl in red Riviera
    1 15½" red Riviera platter
    1 sugar and creamer in green Riviera

Included with this was a promotional poster advertising this set for the sum of $14.95 . . . enough to dazzle the heart of any housewife, whether she were a bride or a grandmother!

Several unusual items have recently been discovered, and we feel must be attributed to the very early years of production before the war scare caused a cut-back. Records were not well kept, especially during these very early years. An example of this are the lids for the nested bowls, recently verified from an illustration in an old trade paper. At least five sizes of these lids have been located, made to fit the #1 through #5 nested bowls.

Early in 1938, a sixth color — turquoise — was chosen to be added to the existing five.

By July 1, 1938, the covered onion soup and the small compartment plate had been dropped from production and the stick handled creamer had been restyled with a ring handle by 1941. There is a 5″ fruit listed on the 1937 list, however by 1939 the listing shows a 5½″ and a 4¾″ fruit. Possibly the 5″ and the 5½″ are the same size fruit, with the so-called 5″ listed actual size in 1939 due to the addition of the 4¾″. In comparing actual measurements to listed measurements, we found variations of as much as ¾″. Assuming the smaller fruit to be the one added in 1939 would account for the scarcity of this item in red — since red was discontinued in 1943 and not made available again until 1959.

Three other items made their first appearance on the 1938 price lists — the 12″ platter, the sauceboat, and the disk water jug.

From 1939 through 1943 the company was involved in a promotional campaign designed to stimulate sales. This involved six special items, each originally offered for sale at 98¢ — the covered refrigerator jars, casserole and pie plate, handled chop plate, French casserole, individual sugar and creamer and tray, and a juice set consisting of a 30 ounce disk pitcher and six 5 ounce tumblers.

These items are not at all easy to find, except for the juice set, which must have been a popular item, since so many are seen yet today. This message was carried on an original flyer from HLC to their distributors.

"JUICE SET IN "FIESTA" . . . To help increase your

sales!" Homer Laughlin is offering an unusual value in the famous Fiesta ware . . . a colorful, 7-piece Juice Set, calculated to fill a real need in the summer refreshment field. The set consists of a 30-oz. disc jug in lovely Fiesta Yellow, and six 5-oz. tumblers, one each in the Fiesta blue, turquoise, red, green, yellow and ivory. Sets come packed one to a carton, and at the one dollar minimum retail price, are sure to create an upward surge in your sales curve. Dealers who take advantage of this Juice Set in Fiesta will find it a potent weapon in increasing sales of other Fiesta items. At a nominal price, customers who have not yet become acquainted with Fiesta, can own some of the ware which has made pottery history during the past few years. The result? They'll want to own more!

Very attractive "bait" that evidently landed many devotees! Although yellow was to have been the standard color for all juice pitchers, several have been found in red, one in grey, and one in light green. It is not, however, totally impossible to find one in some other color due to human error, or because of the whim of an employee with a particular color preference! In so large an operation, this must have occurred many times. We often wondered how the rose color was used for the juice tumblers, since it was not to become a regular Fiesta color for several years. A factory spokesman explained to us that, at this time, the rose glaze had been developed and was already a standard Harlequin color. Since it was available, it was used to add extra color contrast in the juice set. This may also be the reason that a few of the 4¾" fruits are found in medium green.

Occasionally, the juice set is found with a blue-grey pitcher, grey, ivory, and pale pink tumblers. These were dipped to go with a pastel line called Seranade . . . HLC's competition for TS&T's Lu Ray Pastels.

We mentioned in our first book that all of the French casseroles that we had seen were yellow. As with the juice pitchers, yellow was to have been the only color used, and we have never seen any other.

However, one in dark blue has been reported, and a friend has a lid in light green. Again, all individual sugars and creamers were to have been only yellow, and the trays dark blue. But a few red creamers have been found, and several trays in turquoise. Only recently, a sugar was reported in turquoise.

In 1943 our government assumed control of uranium oxide, and as Fiesta red was manufactured from depleted uranium oxide, this color was dropped from production — "Fiesta Red went to war." Perhaps the fact that Fiesta red was always listed separately and priced proportionately higher than the other colors was due, in part, to the higher cost of raw material, plus the fact that the red items required strict control during firing and the losses that did occur had to be absorbed in the final costs.

The color assortment in 1944 included Turquoise, Green, Blue, Yellow, and Old Ivory. The 1944 price list no longer shows the tripod candleholders, nested bowls, or the 10" and 12" flower vases.

Although the colors are listed the same for the 1946 price list, the following pieces were no longer available: Bud vase, bulb type candleholders, carafe, 12" comport, sweets comport, 8" vase, 11½" fruit bowl, ice pitcher, marmalade, mustard, 9½" nappy, footed salad bowl, large tea pot, tumblers, and utility tray.

From 1946 through 1950 we have found no written information nor can the factory provide us with any. Perhaps, at some time during these four years, the color assortment was changed; we can't be sure. However, the October 1, 1951, price list does show these changes, and this may or may not have been the first year for them. Light Green, Navy Blue and Old Ivory were retired from active duty some time after the war was over — and their replacements were Forest Green, Rose, Chartreuse, and Grey, augmented by two old standards, Turquoise and Yellow.

If you have fallen into the habit of referring to these new colors as the "war colors", as we have, they might be more accurately dubbed

"Fifties' colors", since they and the listed assortment remained in production unchanged until 1959.

It is interesting to note, in comparing two 1956 price lists, one designated New Pacific coast retail, that prices were slightly higher on the West coast, probably due to transportation costs.

The big news in 1959 was, of course, the fact that Fiesta Red had finished her patriotic duty and was welcomed back home with much ado! The Atomic Energy Commission licensed The Homer Laughlin China Company to again buy the depleted uranium oxide and Fiesta Red, the most popular of all colors, returned to the market in May of 1959.

In addition to Red, Turquoise and Yellow, Medium Green was offered for the first time. The following items were no longer available:

15″ Chop plate; Coffee cups and saucers, A.D.; Coffee pots, regular; 10½″ compartment plates; Cream soup cups; Egg cups; 4¾″ fruit; 2 pint jug.

A new item makes a first appearance — the individual salad bowl. During the sixties, no changes were made either in the line or with the colors. Though retail prices had risen in 1965, by 1968 some items remained unchanged while others had actually dropped just a little.

In the latter months of 1969, in an effort to meet the needs of the modern housewife and to present a product that was better designed to be in keeping with modern day decor, Fiesta was restyled and only one of the original colors, Fiesta Red, always the favorite, continued in production.

As a footnote, we include a short chapter on Fiesta Ironstone, without which perhaps the story of Fiesta would not be complete. Due to its very contemporary flair and modern colors, however, we feel reluctant to include it in our story, except as a sequel. However, in the days to come — perhaps even now in the minds of some — Fiesta Ironstone will be as collectible as the old line.

IDENTIFICATION OF TRADEMARK, DESIGN AND COLOR

The original design, colors, and name are the registered property of the Homer Laughlin China Company, Patent No. 390-298 was filed on March 20, 1937, having been used by them since November 11, 1935. With only a few exceptions their distinctive trademark appears on every piece. These four seem to be the most common.

fiesta

HLC USA

H. L. C.

fiesta

MADE IN
U.S.A.

fiesta

MADE IN
U.S.A.

GENUINE

fiesta

H. L. Co.   USA
(Handstamped)

The indented trademark was the result of each item being marked in the mold while still in the clay state; the ink mark was put on by a handstamp, after the color was applied and before the final glaze was fired.

As many other manufacturers were following the trend to brightly colored dinnerware, the wide success and popularity of

Fiesta resulted in its being closely copied and produced at one time by another company. The Homer Laughlin Company quickly brought suit against their competitor and forced the imitation ware to be discontinued. Although there are those who contend that Fiesta was made by other manufacturers, "Genuine Fiesta" was the exclusive product of Homer Laughlin.

A novice collector might well be advised to limit himself to marked pieces. However, as one becomes better acquainted with Fiesta, as a general rule, these imitations and the other similar wares are more easily recognized as such.

There are two other patterns which are at first sight easily confused with Fiesta. These are Harlequin and Riviera — not intended as imitations of Fiesta, but rather quite collectible in their own right. These were also made by Homer Laughlin, and we shall bring them to your attention again in another section.

There are some items in the Fiesta line which were never marked — juice glasses, demitasse cups, salt and peppers, and some of the Kitchen Kraft line. The tea cups were never to have been marked as a standard procedure, but a rare few have been found with the ink stamp. We have in our collection two covered onion soups; neither are marked. Never pass up a "goodie" such as these simply because they are unmarked — you may never own one! Sweets comports and ash trays may or may not be marked. As you become aware of the design and its familiar colors, these pieces will be easily identified as Fiesta.

Fiesta's design is very simple and therefore very versatile. The pattern consists of a band of concentric rings graduating in width, with those nearer the rim having the wider space between. The rings are repeated in the center motif on such pieces as plates, nappies, platters, desserts, etc. Handles are applied with slight ornamentation at the base. Flat pieces and bowls are round or oval, hollowware pieces are globular and many are styled with a short pedestal base, which also shows the band of rings.

But of course, it is Fiesta's vivid colors that first catch your attention. The wide array of color provides endless possibilities for matching color schemes and decor. Does Mediterranean best express your personality? Perhaps your choice will be Fiesta Red! Early American? Envision dark blue and grey with your pewter. A sunny breakfast nook becomes even more cheerful with a table set of bright yellow. Or perhaps your taste runs to simple elegance — shades of green and blue place settings, completely accessorized with Old Ivory.

But should you find you love all eleven colors, you'll surely enjoy collecting a place setting in every color — Fiesta Red, Rose, Old Ivory, Grey, Dark Blue, Light Green, Chartreuse, Dark Green, Turquoise, Yellow, and Medium Green. (Shown below, clockwise)

Question:

When is it possible to "see red" and be happy at the same time???

Answer:

   (a) When it's Fiesta Red

   (b) When it's Harlequin Tangerine

   (e) When it's Riviera Red

   (d) *All* of the above!

Score 100% if your answer is (d)

NOW SHOWING . . . SPECIAL ADDED ATTRACTION
THE MEDIUM GREEN ENIGMA!!!

No, we're not talking about a rock group, but one of the most exciting of the Fiesta colors . . . and what makes it so exciting are those items that persistently "pop up" in medium green that we've never found listed on any company records as ever having been produced in that color! Not all of the pieces shown here are "enigmas" — but are never-the-less especially attractive to collectors in this color.

Top Row: 15" and 13" chop plates. Both sizes were in the original assortment. The larger size was discontinued around 1959, while the smaller continued in production until restyling. (We met a former restaurant owner, who told us that he used to send out steak dinners on Fiesta chop plates . . . only a few were returned for the deposit.)

Middle: 11⅝" and 10½" compartment plates. We never yet have found the larger plate listed and they seem to be a little hard to find; since no turquoise has ever been reported, we must assume these plates were in production for a short time before that color was added early in 1938. Not quite so scarce, the smaller size was in the original assortment. It's difficult to find in chartreuse, and was dropped from production before the advent of medium green.

Bottom: 10" dinner plate, 9" luncheon, 7" bread and butter, 6" dessert plate. No shortage here, although 10" dinner plates are not as plentiful as the luncheons. The number of rings on the bottom of a plate identified the jiggerman, for quality control purposes.

Of course, as always, red is at a premium . . . but in some areas, these 50's colors have even out-distanced red!

Top: Deep plate, 8". This original item continued in production until restyling. Of course, it is found in all eleven colors, with red and the 50's colors most desirable.

Middle,
Left: Cream soup cup. These seem to be found without too much searching — watch for slight damage around the area of the handle or the foot. They were dropped by 1959, but a few have been found in medium green!

Center: Individual salad bowl, 7⅝". This was a later piece, not being listed until 1959. Occasionally you may find one with no center rings, probably produced toward the period of transition into Ironstone. Although relatively rare in any color, red and medium green are found more often than turquoise and yellow.

Middle,
Right: 6" dessert bowl. This original piece was dropped around 1959, and medium green is hard to find.

Bottom: 4¾" and 5½" fruits. One of these was the original 5" bowl, the other was added in 1939. We believe the smaller to be the 1939 bowl, due to the scarcity of this item in red. If so, then it would have been produced in red for 4 years only, before Fiesta Red went to war in 1943. Although not appearing on the 1959 price list with the new color assortment, a rare few have been found in medium green.

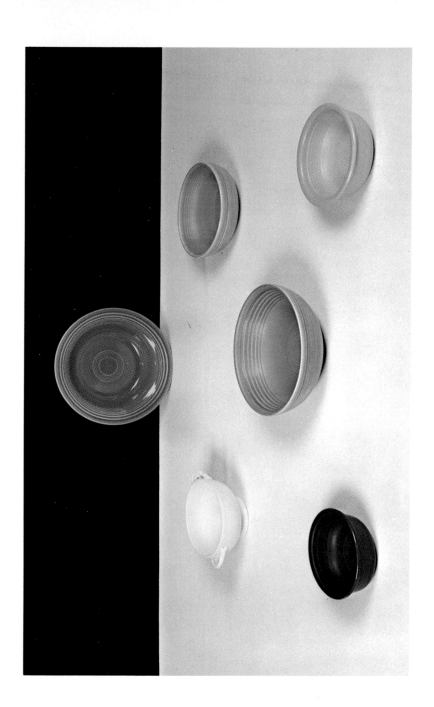

Top: Coffee pot, regular; tea cups and saucers. The coffee server was produced in all Fiesta colors, except med. green, since it was dropped just before 1959 . . . and those 50's colors are almost equal in value to red! Of course tea cups are much in demand. The cups with the inside rings are the older — notice, they also have a hand-turned foot.

Middle: Egg cups. Although this is an original item and continued in production until just before 1959, they are not easily found. Yellow and turquoise are most common, and of the 50's colors, dark green and rose are most in demand . . . no medium green has been reported — yet! Ever wonder about the size? A lady explained this in a letter to us. She said that eggs used to be served poached, in such a large cup as this, so that one might have room to dunk his toast!

Lower
Right: Tom and Jerry mug. These little items are very popular and rising price tags reflect this fact. They were produced in all eleven colors; red ones are at a premium, and here's a surprise — ivory mugs are rare, and on the price scale seem to follow after red. Med. green is next, with the 50's colors led by dark green just behind.

Top: Disk pitcher, 10 oz. tumblers. Not original, but added to the line in 1939, this pitcher continued to be made until 1973. It seemed to be most scarce in chartreuse, followed by med. green, then dark green and rose. Perhaps least compatible with the bright colors of the tumblers, grey seems to be less popular. The tumblers were dropped in 1946, and you will find them only in the original six colors, with turquoise perhaps a little scarce. A friend has seen two ceramic type tiles in old ivory with decals depicting Fiesta. One shows a disk pitcher and a tumbler, while the other shows a coffee server and a tea cup and saucer. Wouldn't that be a "find"!!

Bottom: Sugar and creamer, regular, and stick handled creamer. The stick handled creamer was the original one, and was made in six original colors. It was restyled in 1941 with a ring handle.

Utility tray. An original item produced until 1946 in six original colors. These are in good demand; they're a little hard to find in red.

Salt and peppers. This was another original item that was made until the end. Aside from the larger Kitchen Kraft shakers, these are the only Fiesta shakers. You may find a good imitation, with shaker holes on the side . . . these are not Fiesta.

Top: Platter, 12″. The first listing for this platter is 1939, although it then continued in production until restyling, when it was enlarged to 13″.

9½″ and 8½″ nappies. Both sizes were original; however, the larger size was dropped in 1946. The 8½″ carried through until restyling.

Yellow salad bowl, 9½″. Although never found on company records, a trade paper once reproduced an old ad that offered this bowl complete with salad fork and server for 98¢! Only one has been reported in a color other than yellow . . . it was blue.

Center,
Left: Footed salad bowl. Rather hard to find, this bowl was dropped in 1946, and came only in red, dark blue, Old Ivory, yellow, turquoise, and lgt. green, with ivory and yellow being harder to find.

Bottom,
Right: 11¾″ fruit bowl. This was made for seven years only, between 1939 and 1945, in six original colors. They are quite scarce.

Rarely found in red; turquoise, navy, and ivory are also uncommon.

Top: Nested bowls — 11½″, 10″, 9″, 8″, 7″, 6″, 5″. These bowls, though original, were not found listed by 1944. They are numbered in sequence on the bottom. They are rather scarce, and very heavy! Stacked as a unit they weigh just under 20 lbs.!

#7 has now edged out #1 on the scarcity poll, with #2 and #3 being the most common.

Center,
Left: Sauceboat. A beautifully designed Fiesta piece! Although not original, it was produced from '39 to the end in all colors.

This is a popular piece, and red and the colors of the 50's are increasingly hard to find.

Bottom,
Right: Covered casserole. Considering that production on this item was continuous from 1936, there are not many to be found. The design was completely changed at the restyling.

Hardest to find in med. green and dark green, these colors are often priced with the red!

Top: Relish tray. Five individual sections fit into the base on this very nice piece. You will find these in the six original colors only, since it was discontinued before 1946.

One particularly beautiful example of a Fiesta relish is considered by one collector-dealer-friend to be "the last piece I may ever part with"! Done in ivory, the base is filigreed in gold, and each individual section is decorated with a rose decal! By the way, those center sections may look like coasters, but they weren't produced as such!

12″ comport. This piece is beautiful filled with fruit, or a candle and flowers. Discontinued before 1946, it was of course made only in red, dark blue, lgt. green, yellow, turquoise, and old ivory.

Bottom: Coffee Pot, A.D., cups and saucers. (After dinner). Although production stopped before 1944 on the pot, the demitasse cups and saucers continued until around 1951. The pot was made only in the original six colors; the cups in all but medium green. They are very rare in the rose, chartreuse, dark green, and grey; the pots are harder to find in red, turquoise, and ivory.

Top: Carafe, 3 pt. This item was no longer listed on 1946 price lists. The top has a cork seal. Made only in six colors, its unique shape makes it a favorite among collectors.

Red is not only harder to find, but has "status" appeal; and ivory is also scarce.

Ice pitcher, 2 qt. Dropped before 1946, it was made in red, yellow, old ivory, lgt. green, dark blue and turquoise. Though its looks seem to suggest otherwise, it does not take a lid.

Ivory is the scarce one, although some dealers report low demand for this piece in any color but red.

Bottom: 2 pt. jug. This original item was produced until 1959 and was made in all colors but medium green.

It is most scarce in red, followed by dark green, rose and chartreuse.

Covered onion soup. Why would such a darling item have been the first to go? It wasn't even listed by 1939. As a result, they are very scarce, especially in turquoise. Red and ivory are also harder to find colors; with blue and yellow most common.

Top,

Clockwise: Ash tray, sweets comport, syrup pitcher, marmalade, and mustard. We found that the sweets comport, mustard and marmalade had been discontinued before 1946. (Spoons are not original). Mustards and marmalades are always in demand . . . red mustards are harder to find than red marmalades, and are usually very high! The ash trays were produced from '36-'73. The syrups rate high with collectors, red ones are relatively common, but again that "status" drives the price up! Ivory is the rare color!

Bottom: Tea pot, large, 8 cups; tea pot, medium, 6 cups. The larger tea pot was an original item and was discontinued around 1945, being made, of course, in only the first six colors — red, blue, green, yellow, old ivory, and turquoise. The medium was original and continued to be produced until the line was discontinued.

Top: The 10″ vase was the original size, although by May of '37 all three sizes were listed. By 1944 all had been discontinued but the 8″ vase, and, by 1946, it too was no longer available. All three sizes are very scarce, especially the 10″; the turquoise and ivory are harder-to-find colors. On the other hand, the bud vases, even though dropped before '46 are more readily available. All were produced in six older colors only.

Bottom,
Left: Tripod Candleholders. A pair of these unusual candleholders would be a fine addition to any collection, but they are some of the rarer items in the line. Discontinued around '42 or '43, they were made only in the six original colors.

Bottom,
Right: Bulb type candleholders. Although these were made for only two years longer than the tripods, they are much easier to find. They are available in the same color assortment as the tripods.

These are four of six special promotional items offered by HLC from 1939-43. They were originally offered for sale at 98¢ and were part of a campaign designed to stimulate sales. The other two items included in this campaign were the covered refrigerator jars, and the casserole, which sold with the pie plate. You will see these in the Kitchen Kraft section.

Top: Handled chop plate. This is the 13″ chop plate, fitted with a metal spring handle, one of the few metal accessories shipped directly from HLC. (Very scarce with this handle.)

French casserole. Its unique styling makes this a popular item among collectors. Although not as rare as once thought, they're still quite scarce. Yellow was to have been the standard color, but one has been reported in dark blue, and a lid in light green.

Individual sugar, creamer and tray. This was described to us at the factory as being a yellow sugar and creamer on a dark blue tray, but occasionally you will find a red creamer, and once in awhile a turquoise tray. At least one sugar exists in turquoise.

Bottom: 30 oz. juice pitcher, 5 oz. tumblers. Of the six promotional items, this is the only one that is easy to find. 99% of the pitchers are yellow . . . red ones are rare! Light green has been reported, and a friend has one in grey. We found only recently that the grey was offered in 1952 along with the juice tumblers in "green, (dark green, we assume, since light green was discontinued and medium green was still in the future), yellow, and chartreuse"! Although rose was not a standard color until the 50's it was borrowed from the Harlequin line for contrast as early as 1939.

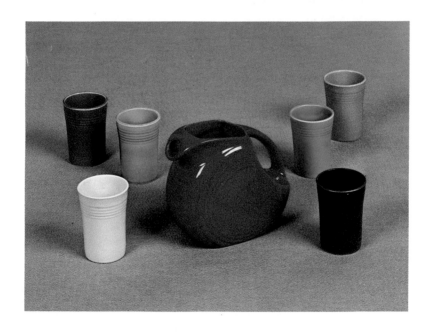

The tiered tidbit trays were not made at HLC, but were drilled and assembled by some other concern. Nor were the metal holders for the marmalades, mustard, salt and peppers ever supplied by Homer Laughlin. The metal holders for the Kitchen Kraft casseroles (7½″ shown), oval platters and pie plates were shipped from the factory as complete units, as were the metal handles for the chop plates.

A collector has sent us a photo of her Fiesta pin-up lamp! Although certainly not of HLC manufacture, it's metal parts were evidently fashioned years ago by a metal company who wisely took advantage of Fiesta's popularity. A 7¾″ plate fits flush against the wall, and a metal tube that conceals the electric cord emerges at the bottom just above the "rings", gracefully curves downward and then straight up, through a cup and saucer . . . the cup holds the light fixture, and the shade decorated with a fruit decal covers the bulb.

The large wooden salad bowl sets on a base banded in Fiesta colors; on the base is a sticker that reads "G. H. Specialty Co., Fiestawood." On the following page you will see a large lazy Susan of the same manufacturer.

The pastel juice set, as well as several of the Kitchen Kraft items, were dipped to go with the Serenade line, HLC's answer to TS&T's Lu Ray Pastels. These are highly prized by many collectors.

The nappy in the metal holder is the 9½″. No information on this, but too many have been found in such a holder as to be coincidental.

The chrome frame for the cream soup converts it very nicely into a jam dish, and the large tea pot becomes a dripolator with the addition of the metal assembly (5½″ high). These were original, although not from HLC. Nor was the wire frame for the juice set, but isn't it nice . . . very functional! Note the chartreuse juice tumbler, . . . very unusual! Look for one in dark green, these were a 1952 issue, part of a juice set with a grey pitcher and a yellow tumbler that completed the set.

This is the Sta-bright flatware, shown in each of four colors, that often accompanied accessorized sets of Fiesta. One collector reports swizzle sticks with her set!

The large (20″ wide) lazy Susan is another Fiestawood piece by G. H. Specialty Co.

These items are often marked with this ink stamp:

HOLLYWOOD
MERRY-GO-ROUND
Copyright 1936
G. H. SPECIALTY CO.
MILWAUKEE, WIS.

We have received photos of a holder for the Fiesta nappy in natural wood decorated with three bright hand painted red tomatoes, but with no mark to indicate the manufacturer.

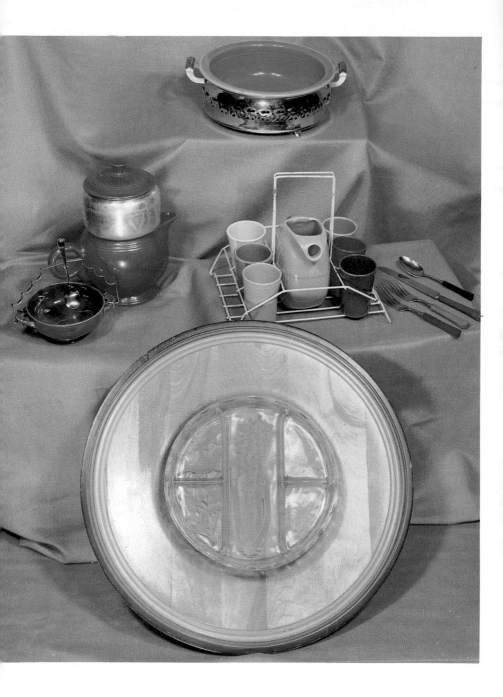

Top: Tom and Jerry set. This is the large salad bowl and the Tom & Jerry mugs, with gold bands and lettering. It's a beautiful set, and our friends to whom it belongs tell us they bought it for a "song" . . . stuck back under a table at an Antique Show!

Few complete sets have been located, mugs are more common than the bowls.

Middle: Two advertising pieces, in this case Tom & Jerrys advertising Pure Oil and O.K. Trucking. Both are very nice! The color of these mugs is white . . . not ivory!

Left: Homer Laughlin was quick to deny ever having had anything to do with these striped plates. Can you blame them! As you can see, they are not underglazed, and the stripes are usually very worn.

Top: The tall mugs in the top row are from a line of HLC hotel china, but note the Fiesta handle. The Sit 'n Sip sets are shown in the bottom row — the advertising mug with matching coaster — along with an original carton. The first mug on the second row is decorated with nursery characters.

Bottom: In addition to the turquoise and rose interiors shown, amberstone, turf green, and yellow have been found. The exterior glaze is white, not ivory! These were produced during the late 60's, into the early 70's. The bottom row are examples of a series decorated with decals of antique automobiles . . . six have been reported: 1924 Model "48" Buick, 1904 Model "B" Buick, 1936 Buick "Special", 1941 Buick Roadmaster, 1908 Model "10" Buick, 1916 Model "D" Buick. From 1964 through 1970 these Sit 'n Sip sets were issued for annual meetings of Buick Management, and their Salaried retirement club meetings. The collector that supplied this information also tells us that she has an ashtray dated 1963, Buick Management Meeting, Dec. 11-12. It is 8¾" round, raised in the center with six cigarette slots. Specialty items and advertising pieces are very popular with today's collector.

Top: This 15″ chop plate has been decorated by a smaller china company; both the decals and the gold trim are applied over the glaze. It's stamped "Vogue China". This Tom and Jerry set has lately been the center of much attention. We didn't include it in previous editions since we have concentrated mainly on the dinnerware lines of HLC . . . and since the other T & J set sported Fiesta shapes, it became the "star", while this one was sadly neglected. But not by all of you! As many of you have pointed out, this set is also quite lovely and should at least deserve an introduction!

Bottom: Another Fiesta wood piece, this large tray measures 16½″. The ash tray is one we hunted for several years. On our first trip to HLC in 1972, we saw one on display, stamped in gold, as this one is, "1939, East Liverpool, Ohio, Rotary Club". We advertised for one in local papers while we were there to no avail, and had completely given up ever locating one when a lady from the East Liverpool area wrote, offering this one for trade. The metal lazy susan stand has a ball bearing section in between the disks that allows the top to rotate. The width of that flat rim fits between the rings under some 13″ and 15″ chop plates. This is another example of accessories made by companies other than HLC. The wood and metal handle nicely converts a Fiesta tumbler into a soda fountain mug . . . not of HLC manufacture.

Top: These commemorative pieces were made for the Lazarus Company, who issued them from 1938 through 1941 on their anniversary. Plates and tumblers may also be found.

Middle: This is the 15″ chop plate and a 7″ plate with a multi-floral decal in the center and the maroon rings around the rims. It is stamped "Fiesta" and is very rare.

The turkey decal is shown here on the 13″ chop plate. You may find it also on the 15″ size, as well as the dinner plate. This is an under-glaze decoration on commercial quality, according to HLC. These are very rare, also.

A lovely set consisting of the large chop plate and six salad plates was reported last year. In the area of the center rings the large plate was decorated with decals of dancers in colonial costumes, the salad plates depict a colonial gentleman kneeling before a lady who is seated. The remaining area on each plate was decorated with an overall cherry pattern in gold. Each piece was stamped Genuine Fiesta, HLC, USA, and Royal China, Warranteed, 22 Kt. Gold.

Bottom: The Homer Laughlin China Company issued a calendar plate for a number of years, using whatever blanks were available. In 1954 and 1955 they just happened to use Fiesta. The 9″ plate is the rare one . . . the 1954 plate has been found in ivory only, the '55 in green, yellow and ivory.

Top: This beautiful place setting of decaled Fiesta is part of a complete service. A lovely lady who loves Fiesta loaned it to us to show you. She is needing only a few pieces to replace some that are damaged. Please let us know if you have any. Another lucky collector sent photos of her set . . . multifloral central decal, accented with a burgandy stripe at the rim. Sets such as these are very rare! She also mentioned a set in red trimmed with gold and stamped 24 K Gold.

Bottom,
Left: This is the large footed salad bowl, decorated inside and out with lovely floral decals and piped in green . . . absolutely fantastic! (These decals and those on the dinnerware above are under-glazed, and were of course applied by the factory.)

Bottom,
Right: This 10" cake plate is completely flat and is very, very rare!

Top,
Left to Right: This creamer is 4″ high and was most probably experimental. The very unusual comport is only 10″ x 2½″ high. Next is the base section of the experimental individual tea pot we found in the morgue. We would have loved to show it with the lid, which is interchangeable with the A.D. pot, but this particular one was just enough "off-round" that our lid would not fit.

Bottom: These are unusual colors for the individual creamer and tray . . . both must be considered scarce, although not as extremely rare as we once thought. Only one sugar has been reported in any color other than the standard yellow; it is turquoise.

The box containing a creamer features the Fiesta dancing girl. Advertising pieces such as this one are creating quite a stir!

The medium green small fruits are rare; the red relish section was designed so that four would fit a large oval tray — strictly experimental!

74

Top: Paper items — especially advertising material — make interesting additions to our collections, and are really worthy investments! We wanted to show you the cover of this Saturday Evening Post, September 1939, so that if the date escapes you, you will recognize this issue when you see it. Inside is a beautiful two-page Armstrong Floor covering ad with a vintage kitchen-dining room fairly blooming with Fiesta. (We would have photographed it for you, but a certain party, who shall remain name-less ruined her copy trying to decoupage it without first reading the instructions). The company's price lists not only contain much information, but are in themselves collectors items. The menu and the corn package are examples of the influence of HLC's lines in commercial work. The toothpaste ad in the March '78 issues of McCalls, Better Homes, uses a beautiful display of blue Fiesta. The sheet of decals were produced in 1945 by a company called American Decalcomania of Chicago and New York, and sold for 29¢ per sheet of six designs. The glass decanter shown in two designs has been found, and is marked "Nolen Austin Co., Feb. 1942, Glasbake, Pat. U.S.A." Look for these magazines for articles with photos of Fiesta: House Beautiful, Aug., 1976; Mainliner, United Airlines, Sept., '76; Apartment Living, Jan., '76; and House and Garden, Feb., '77.

Bottom: The canister set and the napkin holder are tin, decorated with Fiesta-like dinnerware, of the type popular during the late 1930's and early 40's. The American Home, Oct., 1938 carried on article called "Pretty Up Your Kitchen" which featured not only Fiesta, but tinware by Owens-Illinois Can Co. decorated in "Roman stripes in red, blue, and green on yellow". The set consisted of canisters, tray, bread box, dust pan and garbage can, and it, too, was called "Fiesta".

Top: This "Fiesta Egg Cooker" was produced by The Hankscraft Company in 1942 and was sold alone for $4.95 or in the "Fiesta Egg Service Set" which included a "gleaming chrome and clear maple" tray and "four vari-colored Fiesta egg cups" and "Fiesta salt and pepper shakers" for $9.50. Now the problem is this! Although the ad stresses the words "Genuine Fiesta" and sure enough shows "Genuine Fiesta", the sets that are so often reported are like this one . . . and those are certainly anything but "Genuine Fiesta" egg cups! We vaguely remember reading a letter from someone who had written to a popular collector's paper explaining that Hankscraft offered two such sets . . . one "standard" and one "deluxe"??? can anyone help??? The Hazel-Atlas poaching dish is a hard to find part of the set!

Bottom: HLC look-alikes! As we've tried to impress on new collectors, examine and study everything well before jumping to conclusions. We've included this photo to emphasize the point! On the right is a "Fiesta bud vase" that is not a Fiesta bud vase . . . but a copy of one. Aside from the obviously inferior glaze, the piece is just enough smaller to indicate that it has been made from a mold taken from an original. The disk pitcher is not!!! (and as Baretta would say, "dat's the name of dat tune"!) The cake plate, while very beautiful, is not Fiesta . . . the donkey may look like its Harlequin double, but sometimes pulls a cart marked "California"! A "dead ringer" without rings, the last pitcher looks very much like the Harlequin novelty creamer. Beware!

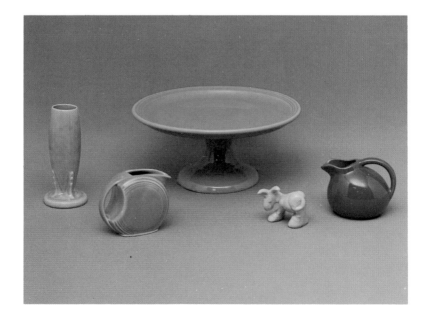

Top: We thought these nested mixing bowls were especially nice. The orange tree pattern is very similar to the one used by Fenton! They're marked with the HLCo mark.

Bottom: Sure to become a "must" on everyone's "want list", this HLC child's set is beautifully done in colorful detailed decals on ivory. This set and many other items often carry an ink stamped series of letters and numbers; the Company has provided this information that should be of help to you in deciphering these codes:

"In 1900 the trademark featured a single numeral identifying the month, a second single numeral identifying the year and a numeral 1, 2, or 3 designating the point of manufacture as East Liverpool, Ohio.

In the period 1910-20, the first figure indicated the month of the year, the next two numbers indicated the year, and the third figure designated the plant. Number 4 was "N", Number 5 was "N5", and the East End plant was "L".

A change was made for the period of 1921-1930. The first letter was used to indicate the month of the year such as "A" for January, "B" for February, "C" for March. The next single digit number was used to indicate the year and the last figure for the plant.

For the period 1931-40 the month was expressed as a letter, but the year was indicated with two digits. Plant No. 4 was "N", No. 5 was "R", No. 6 and 7 were "C", and No. 8 was listed as "P". During the period, E-44R5 would indicate May of 1944 and manufactured by Plant No. 5. The current trademark has been in use for approximately 70 years, and the numbers are the only indication of the year that items were produced."

THE FIESTA CASUALS
GENUINE

H. L. Co. USA
CASUAL

There were two designs produced in the beautiful Fiesta Casuals; and although they are both relatively difficult to find, often, when they are available, the set may be complete, or nearly so.

They were first introduced in June, 1962; and, as sales were only moderately active, they were discontinued around 1968. The Plaid Stamp Company featured both of these designs in their illustrated catalogues during these years.

The Hawaiian 12-Point Daisy design, No. F-108, featured a ½" turquoise band at the rim, and turquoise daisies with brown centers on a white background.

The other design was Yellow Carnation, No. F-107, which featured the yellow flowers with a touch of brown on the white background and with yellow piping at the rim. In both instances only the dinner plates, salad plates, saucers and oval platters were decorated; the cups, fruit dishes, nappies, and sugar and creamers were simply the matching Fiesta color.

Using a lead mask with the cut-out design, the decoration was hand-sprayed and overglazed. A complete service consisted of six place settings: dinner plate, salad plate, cup and saucer, and fruit (5½"). A platter, 8½" nappy, and the sugar and creamer were also included.

AMBERSTONE

This "brown Fiesta" seems to have caused quite a stir among our collector friends; and it's easy to see why . . . especially when some of the hollowware pieces are found with the familiar Fiesta cast-indented trademark!

Amberstone was introduced in 1967, three years before the Fiesta line was restyled; yet the illustration on an old order blank shows that the sugar and creamer, cup, tea pot, soup/cereal, casserole, and coffee server were from the same molds that were later used for the Fiesta Ironstone. Only on the pieces that had relatively flat areas large enough to permit decoration do you find the black, machine-stamped underglazed pattern. The remainder were solid brown glazed.

Sold under the trade name of Genuine Sheffield dinnerware, it was produced by HLC exclusively for supermarket promotions, and several large grocery chains featured Amberstone as a premium. These items were offered, and for your information we have indicated those having the design with an asterisk:

Dinner Plate*
Dessert Dish
Bread & Butter*
Coffee Cup
Saucer*
Vegetable Bowl
Covered Sugar Bowl
Creamer
Oval Platter, 13"*
Large Soup Plate*
Ash Tray
Salt & Pepper Shakers
Salad Plate*

Soup/Cereal Bowl
Covered Casserole
Sauce Boat
Relish Tray*
Coffee Server
Tea Server
Covered Butter Dish, (stick)
Round Serving Platter*
Jumbo Salad Bowl
Covered Jam Jar
Serving Pitcher (disk)
Jumbo Mug
Pie Plate*

CASUALSTONE

In 1970, Homer Laughlin again produced a line of dinnerware to be sold exclusively as supermarket promotions. This dinnerware was called Casualstone, and was presented under the trade name "Coventry". The Antique Gold of the Fiesta Ironstone was decorated with an intricate gold machine stamped design and, as with Amberstone, it appeared on only the shallow items.

An old order blank shows that it was less expensive than the Amberstone of three years previous . . . and in these days of ever increasing inflation it was refreshing to notice this! But quite possibly this was due to the fact that a standard color was used. The following pieces were available; those with the design are indicated by an asterisk:

Dinner Plate*	Dessert Dish
Coffee Cup	Saucer*
Bread & Butter*	Round Vegetable Bowl
Covered Sugar Bowl	Creamer
13" Oval Platter*	Soup Plate*
Ash Trays	Salt and Pepper
Salad Plates*	Soup/Cereal Bowls
Covered Casserole	Sauce Boat
Relish Tray*	Coffee Server
Tea Server	Covered Butter Dish (stick)
Round Platter*	Jumbo Salad Bowl
Covered Jam Jar	Pitcher
Jumbo Mugs	Pie Plate*

FIESTA IRONSTONE

In 1969, Fiesta was restyled and the line that was offered in February 1970, was then called Fiesta Ironstone. There were many factors that, of necessity, brought this change about. Labor and production costs had risen sharply. Efforts to hold these costs down resulted in the use of two new colors which were, and still are, standard colors for several other lines of dinnerware produced at HLC, Antique Gold and Turf Green. This eliminated the need of a separate firing that had been necessary for the older Fiesta colors. It was pointed out to us as we toured the factory that since each color required different temperatures in the kiln, orders were running ahead of production on Fiesta as well as their other lines.

In order to cut labor costs, all markings were eliminated.

The restyled pieces had a more contemporary feeling — bowls were flared; the applied handles were only partial rings. The covered casserole had molded, closed handles and the sugar bowl was without handles. The covered coffee server made a return appearance after an absence of several years.

Nineteen items were offered in three colors, Antique Gold, Turf Green, and the original red . . . now called Mango Red.

The oval platter was enlarged to 13″; two new items were offered, the sauceboat stand and a 10¼″ salad bowl.

Finally in November, 1972, all production of Fiesta Red was discontinued because many of the original technicians who developed this color and maintained control over the complicated manufacturing and firing had retired and modern mass production methods were unsuited to the process.

Then at last, on January 1, 1973, the famous line of Fiesta Dinnerware was discontinued.

FIESTA KITCHEN KRAFT

Since the early 1930's the Homer Laughlin China Company had been well known as manufacturers of a wide variety of ceramic kitchen wares.

In 1939 they introduced a bake and serve line called Fiesta Kitchen Kraft, as an extension of their already popular genuine Fiesta ware. This they offered in the four original Fiesta colors — red, yellow, green and blue. The following pieces were available: (Compiled from April, 1941, price list)

Covered Jars, small, medium and large
Large covered Jug
Mixing Bowls — 10", 8", and 6"
Spoon, Fork and Cake Server
Covered Casseroles, 8½", 7½", and individual
4 piece refrigerator set
Pie plate, 10"
Cake plate, 11"
Large salt and pepper shakers
Plates, 6" and 9"

These were chosen from the standard assortment of Kitchenware items which had been the basis of the many Kitchen Kraft and Oven Server decaled lines of years previous; none were created especially for Fiesta Kitchen Kraft.

This line was in production for a relatively short period, through the early '40's — perhaps being discontinued during the Second World War prior to 1945.

As collectors are becoming more aware of its identity, more of these Fiesta Kitchen Kraft items are becoming available. You undoubtedly know if you have collected it, it is by no means easily found, and prices are usually very high.

There were two standard marks used for this line — the cast indented mark and the paper label. Naturally, many of these paper labels were removed, and, as a result you will find many pieces are not marked. Occasionally you may find a third mark, simply Fiesta . . . hand stamped in gold ink.

In addition to the items listed previously, there are at least three more to add. These may have been offered in the original assortment and discontinued by the 1941 listing. The first of these to come to our attention was the oval platter. As with the casserole, it was supplied with a chrome holder, and shipped from the factory as a complete unit. There was also a chrome holder for the 10″ pie plate. A second size pie plate measuring 9″ has also been found. Although unmarked, it, too, is an easily recognizeable HLC mold, and is often found with decals in this size. As a good example of the durability of this kitchen ware, a good friend tells us of a relative who has used her pie plate once or twice a week for over thirty years, and it is still in very good condition!

The third new item is actually only a variation of one of those already listed, and has probably been the basis of more confusion and more questions than any other piece HLC ever made . . . and that is a second size Kitchen Kraft covered jug! The difference in size is so slight, even side by side it could go unnoticed — and to be honest, we don't know which size was the first, or which is the hardest to find. Collectors report as many of one size as the other. If you really want to label yours small or large, here are some measurements that will help you.

LARGE		SMALL
21½″	circumference	20″
5⅛″	base rim	4¾″
3¾″	rim inside lid	3⅜″
2⅜″	diameter of knob	2¼″

The 6" and 9" plates listed on the 1941 illustrated brochure, may have been used as underplates for the hot casseroles. When we visited the morgue at HLC, we saw what must have been an example of these — they were of a thinner gauge and seemed to have been taken from one of their other lines, since the style was not typical . . . they were round and had a moderately wide, slightly flared rim.

If you have been interested at all in the decaled lines, you are probably familiar enough with the Kitchen Kraft molds, that you recognize them at first glimpse. Several collectors have mentioned finding the stack set, salt and peppers, mixing bowls and other items with an ivory glaze. We have seen some in the blue-grey. The company tells us that these were dipped to go with their pastel line, Serenade. This was offered by HLC to compete with TS&T's Lu Ray Pastels . . . and the Kitchen Kraft mixing bowls have been reported in Harlequin colors.

Bottom: Covered refrigerator jars. A unit consists of three stacking parts, with a flat lid . . . it's usually made up of all four Kitchen Kraft colors in the unit. This one is special!

Covered jugs! The smaller one stands 5⅞" tall, the **larger** 6¼". These are difficult to find in either size.

Trademarks:

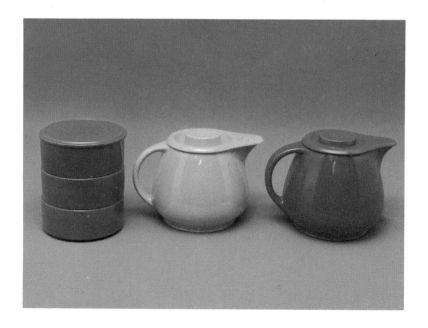

Top: Casseroles, 8½", 7½", and individual. All sizes are very scarce; the small one is especially attractive to collectors, and they are usually priced quite high.

Middle: Covered jars; large, medium and small. Circumferences graduate from 27½" to 22", to 17¼" on the small one. We now have three large jars — one blue, one red and one yellow — which we use as canisters . . . and lovely though they are, they just aren't very handy! (Think I'll change my flour from dark blue to yellow . . . just thinking about that white flour all over my blue jar is enough to discourage all pie baking . . .) All sizes are scarce, but the larger ones are more often found.

Bottom: These mixing bowls measure 10", 8", and 6", and again have proven to be very difficult to find. Note the original sticker on the large one.

Top: Cake plate. These may or may not be marked; the only decoration is the narrow band around the edge formed by one inverted ring.

Pie plates, 10″, 9″. The pie plates were produced without rings, either inside or outside, and are usually not marked. We have one with a gold ink stamp. The small size is very unusual to have been done in the Fiesta colors. This mold was more often decorated with decals.

Middle: On the left is the 10″ pie plate in the metal holder. The casserole in the center is the 8½″ and is shown in the metal holder, as shipped from HLC.

On the far right is the 13″ oval platter, one of the new "finds". These are extremely rare, and probably not marked. Of course, not all of these items were shipped with a metal holder.

Bottom: Spoon, fork and cake server. All are rated highly by collectors, and are not easily found. The handles are decorated with the same embossed flowers as one of the Oven Serve lines.

Salt and Peppers. Larger replicas of their original counterpart, although by no means as plentiful.

HARLEQUIN

Harlequin is a fascinating pattern, abundant with beautiful interesting pieces, as its many enthusiastic fans will be quick to tell you! Although it was first listed on company records in 1936, Harlequin was not introduced to the public until 1938. It was quite popular and sold very well into the late fifties when sales began to diminish. Records show that the final piece was actually manufactured in 1964.

Harlequin was produced by Homer Laughlin in their effort to serve all markets. It was a less expensive, thinner ware, and was sold without trademark exclusively by F. W. Woolworth Co. Stores.

The glaze was similar to Fiesta's, and all of Fiesta's lovely colors were used except ivory . . . but only a few rare pieces were made in dark blue. In addition, there was maroon, a mauve blue, and a "Blue Spruce" shade of green. Officially, the color we call "red" in Fiesta is "Tangerine" in the Harlequin line, and we learned from a retired employee that during some of the war years when uranium oxide was not available to make the standard red glaze, some Harlequin and Riviera was produced by means of a colored stain. The yellow is "Harlequin Yellow", according to the records, and the mauve simply blue. The "spruce" green color was called dark green, and was the original green, and they called the deep maroon shade "red"! If all this seems a bit confusing, may we suggest that to simplify matters (unless you are a purist, in which case "Good Luck"!) we collectors continue to call the Fiesta red shade "red", the spruce green shade "spruce green" rather than dark green since that name is commonly held to be interchangeable with Forest Green, the maroon color "maroon" rather than red which might just avoid an international incident if a Fiesta red fan were to get a maroon marmalade through a mail order instead of one in her beloved red! While your head is still spinning, may we add that although previously we felt that rose and salmon were one and the same, a recent conversation with an HLC spokesman revealed that there was once a shade called salmon — it was discontinued prior to the early 50's — and the rose color was a Harlequin 50's color, as it was in the

Fiesta line. We've never seen any Harlequin in a color that might qualify as salmon, have you? So perhaps until we do, our pink Harlequin should remain "rose".

The following is an excerpt from one of the company's original illustrated brochures:

> *"The new Harlequin Pottery offers a gift to table gaiety. It brings the magic of bright, exciting color to the table, dresses the festive board with pleasantness and personality, makes of every meal a cheerful and companionable occasion.*
>
> *The new ware comes in four lovely colors . . . Yellow, Green, Red, and Blue . . . and offers the hostess endless possibilities for creating interesting and appealing color effects on her table. All the colors are brilliant and eye-catching . . . designed to go together effectively in any combination the hostess may desire. To set a table with Harlequin is an adventure in decoration. Plates are of one color, cups of another, saucers and platters of another . . . you can give free range to your artistic instincts.*
>
> *And it is very easy to build up a comprehensive set of Harlequin in whatever items and colors you desire, because it may be bought by the piece at extremely reasonable prices.*
>
>

Sold Exclusively by
F. W. WOOLWORTH CO. STORES"

The style of Harlequin is pure Art Deco. As with the Fiesta, the pattern consists of a band of concentric rings; however, on Harlequin these rings are spaced away from the rim by a plain margin, whereas with Fiesta the band is placed at the rim. Flat pieces are round and slightly concave, and there is no center motif. Many of the bowls are flared and complement the cone shape of the hollow-ware pieces. Handles are applied, slightly ornate at the base, and all are extremely angular with the exception of the service water jug and its twin in miniature, the novelty creamer.

The original line consisted of these items:

    10" plate
    9" plate
    8" soup plate
    7" plate
    6" plate
    Salt and pepper shakers
    Cream soup cup
    9" nappy
    Sauceboat
    Covered Casserole
    A.D. (After Dinner) coffee cup and saucer
    Novelty creamer
    Tea cup and saucer
    Creamer, regular
    Sugar bowl
    13" platter
    11" platter
    Tea pot
    Service water jug
    36's bowl
    5½" fruit
    Ash tray
    36's oatmeal
    Double egg cup
    Individual salad bowl
    22 oz. jug
    4½" tumbler

The only written material the factory could provide, aside from the original brochure, is dated May 10, 1952. It lists both available and discontinued items, many of which were added to the original assortment over the intervening years.

Listed as discontinued:

> Baker, 7″ (in the pottery trade, a baker is an oval vegetable)
> Cov'd butter
> Marmalade, cov'd
> Individual nut bowl
> Individual Creamer
> Tankard
> Relish Tray
> Individual egg cup

There are three more items that round out the list of unusual Harlequin pieces . . . one is a "new discovery"!

The first is the ash tray saucer, the second a large cup . . . evidently the "tankard" on the discontinued list. It is styled with no rings and the sides are slightly curved rather than straight. It fits nicely into the ash tray saucer; in fact, a factory spokesman is sure they were intended to be used together.

The "new discovery" is a miniature creamer, 2¼″ tall . . . no rings — no angular lines — nothing to hint "Harlequin" except the colors! In a matching nut cup it looks like a tiny pitcher and bowl set, and a few dried star flowers and some status would make a dainty arrangement! The company calls this their individual creamer, so that rare creamer with the high lip will have to relinquish that title . . . now, what will we call that one???

Although it was originally thought to be a Fiesta item, we know now that the elusive spoon rest was indeed made in the Harlequin colors, and as part of this line, was sold through Woolworth's. Also included were a series of small what-nots in the shapes of animals. There were six of these . . . a fish, donkey, duck, lamb, cat and penguin, and considering the furor they have aroused, in this edition they have earned their own section!

Top: 10″ plate in spruce, 9″ in rose, 7″ in mauve, and 6″ in turquoise. Only the larger might be less than plentiful.

Center: Platters, 13″ and 11″.

Bottom: 8″ soup plate, 36's oatmeal shown in med. green, 6½″, 5½″ fruit, and cream soup.

The 36's oatmeal may be a little hard to find, and although the cream soups are around, they seem to be scarce in dark green, grey, rose and chartreuse.

Note: The small incised letters and/or numbers sometimes found on the bottom of hollowware pieces were used to identify a pieceworker . . . perhaps a molder or a trimmer . . . and were used for quality control purposes. More likely to appear on Harlequin, nevertheless these are sometimes seen on Fiesta as well.

Opposite: 9" nappy in red, 36's bowl in yellow, 9" oval baker in mauve blue, 7" individual salad bowl, here shown in grey.

The casserole is a beautiful example of the styling in the Harlequin line; and, although you might have to search for awhile for one, they are to be found.

As a general rule, you will find less med. green, chartreuse, grey, and dark green in the Harlequin line . . . and the casserole is no exception — it's scarce in these colors, too. Rose and red Harlequin seem to be in ample supply. The 36's bowl is very hard to find in rose, grey, chartreuse, med. green and dark green; and the individual salad bowls are scarce in dark green, rose and red.

Top: Notice the band of rings near the bottom on the water jug. This will help you identify this jug as Harlequin. Shown with the water tumblers . . . doesn't it make a beautiful set? As you can plainly see . . . the band of rings are spaced away from the rim by a plain margin, whereas, on the Fiesta tumblers, the rings are at the rim. This has caused some confusion, and often collectors of one pattern have been disappointed with mail orders, when tumblers of the other pattern have been mistakenly represented. Harlequin tumblers are harder to find than Fiesta tumblers. To our knowledge, neither pitcher or tumblers have been found in grey, chartreuse or med. green, and they're quite scarce in light green, rose and maroon.

Bottom: Tea pot, tea cups and saucers. Aren't the cups elegant! There's just no way to hold that dainty handle, without having your "pinkie" automatically extend just a little!

Top: Sugar with cover, and regular creamer, salt and pepper. To the left are two unusual creamers. We used to call these individual creamers! Now that we have a positive I.D. on the "individual" creamer, what term shall we use?? Suggest something! In the meantime, this "high-lip" creamer is 3″ high . . . notice the difference in the length of the lips on the two shown. This is due to the fact that it was trimmed by hand. These are very hard to find! The novelty creamer is shown in red, you'll rarely find it in med. green, chartreuse, dark green or grey. The maroon piece is the marmalade; yellow and turquoise are common; spruce, red, rose, and mauve are harder to come by.

Bottom: Sauceboat; tumbler with decal of antique car is one of a set of 6, decorated by Pearl China. The 22 oz. jug on the left is especially hard to find in dark green, medium green, grey and chartreuse.

Top: The maroon ash tray-saucer combination is shown on the far left. These are very hard to find. Above, in turquoise, is the little basketweave nut dish. At the top of the photo is the rare Harlequin syrup . . . only a few are known to exist. Below it is the ash tray. Note that the rings on this pattern are inside the bowl, rather than on the top rim as Fiesta's are. The large cup, or tankard, is shown to the right of the ash tray. These are very rare. Although we once thought the basketweave ash tray was only an experimental item, too many have been found to support this idea. Chartreuse and dark green are scarce colors, but "status" red tops the price scale.

The little perfume bottle was a specially-made item for a cosmetic company. The butter dish, shown in spruce, originally was part of the Century line, and was dipped in Harlequin colors to be sold with this line and Riviera. These colors are available: cobalt blue, rose, mauve, spruce, light green, maroon, turquoise, "Tangerine" red, yellow and ivory.

Bottom: 5 part relish tray. The base is identical to the Fiesta relish tray, only the rings are slightly altered. It is really a beautiful piece!

Strangely enough, the only true Harlequin bases have been turquoise! When another color is used, they have been done on Fiesta bases!

To the right is an example of a common practice . . . some enterprising company turned a 36's bowl into a nut dish, with the addition of a little chrome and a glass knob!

Recently, a collector sent us a photo of the first Harlequin tiered tid-bit we've heard of . . . very nice!

Top: Double egg cups, here shown in chartreuse, are not hard to find, except in the rare colors, but red ones are becoming scarce. The individual egg cup, shown in spruce, was in production only a short time . . . probably because the stems were hand turned and trimmed . . . and are quite rare. The Harlequin candleholders, too, are rare. The A.D. (after dinner) cups and saucers are styled exactly like the tea cups, and are becoming hard to find — extremely so in dark green, grey and chartreuse.

Bottom: Spoon rests have always created quite a stir (absolutely no pun intended). We thought at first they belonged to the Fiesta family, but later we learned that they were Harlequin. Then, if there was any remaining doubt about it, this beautiful turquoise example was found with its "Harlequin" label intact! The second one is white . . . an advertising item! They measure 8¼" × 6¼".

Top: This wire frame donkey carries Harlequin salt and peppers in his saddlebags — not a HLC product, but cute! In the center is the petite newcomer to the line, the individual creamer. It's 2¼" high and you'll find them in turquoise, mauve blue, spruce green, maroon, yellow, light green, red, and rose. The metal holder turns the tumbler into a tall mug.

Bottom: The cup is the rare tankard, and although the saucer is much larger than the standard Rhythm saucer (this one is 6⅞") the styling is identical. Probably one of a kind, the lamp in the center has a base from a large Fiesta comport, a body of two Harlequin casseroles, and the neck is a small Fiesta comport stem. The Harlequin pamphlet introduces the new line, but lists no prices or assortment. It does name the original colors, yellow, green (spruce), red (maroon) and blue (mauve). Although today we all seem to prefer matching cups and saucers, the pamphlet suggests the buyers be more adventurous . . . it recommends "cups of one color, saucers of another."

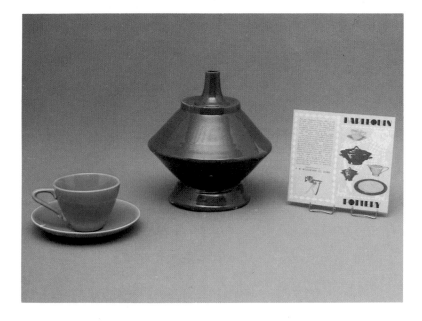

HARLEQUIN ANIMALS

This menagerie of darling animals is part of the Harlequin line. They were sold through F. W. Woolworth Co. Stores during the late 30's, perhaps very early in the 40's, when miniatures such as these were enjoying a hey-day. They are quite rare! For our photography session, a whole herd of the animals arrived — each of the six represented in all four colors . . . maroon, spruce, mauve and yellow . . . plus gold, and white with gold trim!

In the top photo are the original HLC Harlequin animals in authentic glazes. There are no others, although this wee clique has been besieged by hordes of little deer, elephants, other ducks — even a cart — trying to squirm into line. True, the little duck has a double — a perpetually hungry little gander, his head bent into a permanent feeding position — but he was made by the Brush Pottery Company! And although several collectors were almost sure their 2½″ elephant was a "charter member", HLC disowned him! The cart we mentioned is pulled by a donkey "look-alike" (but a second look shows an uncharacteristic lack of sharp detail) and has been found to occasionally bear a "California" mark!

The bottom photo displays the "Maverick" animals . . . a most appropriate term adopted by collectors to indicate animals that have been altered by someone outside the Homer Laughlin China Company. Those in the double row at the bottom are of the same size as the original animals. In some cases, the gold finish or the gold and white finish has been applied over a Harlequin colored glaze. One company involved in decorating the animals was Kaulware, of Chicago, who utilized an iridescent glaze and gold hand painted trim. On the top row of the bottom photo are examples of salt and pepper shakers of a slightly smaller size, which indicates they have been made from molds made from the original animals . . . in fact one of the penguins is a bit smaller than the other.

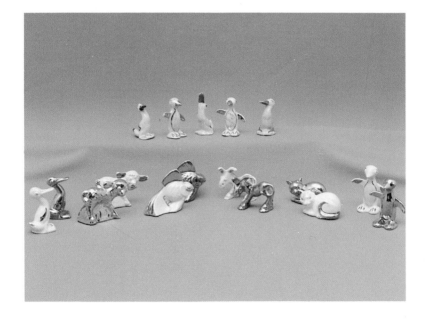

RIVIERA

Riviera was introduced by HLC in 1938 and was sold exclusively by the Murphy Co. In contrast to Fiesta and Harlequin, the line was quite limited. It was unmarked, lighter weight, and therefore less expensive. Very rarely, a piece may be found with the Homer Laughlin gold ink stamp.

Of the three colored dinnerware lines, Riviera has the rather shaky distinction of being the only one which was not originally created as such. Its forerunner was a line called Century — an ivory line with a vellum glaze. Century shapes were also decorated with a wide variety of decals and were the basis of many lines, such as Mexicana and Hacienda. The butter dish was used in the Virginia Rose pattern. An enterprising designer applied the popular colored glazes to these same shapes, and Riviera was born! Even the shakers were taken from another line. They were originally designed as Tango — which accounts for the six section design in contrast to the square Riviera shape.

Riviera is in very short supply, and much to the chagrin of Riviera collectors everywhere, mint condition pieces are very few indeed. Especially bad to chip, were the flat pieces . . . plates, platters, saucers, and undersides of lids. Still, when it is found with no chips, the glaze is nearly always in beautiful condition.

The style is very functional . . . the cups especially so. It is square and somewhat squatty, yet it has so much quaint charm. Certainly Riviera will endear itself to many!

Colors are mauve blue, red, yellow, light green and ivory. On rare occasions dark blue pieces are found . . . but this was never listed as a standard Riviera color. However, there is one thing we have learned — anything is apt to turn up, color-wise! Vats containing upwards of fourteen different colors were all around. Human error and innovation resulted in many unusual things!

Records for this line are especially scanty; but, as accurately and completely as possible, here is a listing of the items in the line as it was first introduced:

8″ dish (platter)
10″ dish (platter)
8″ plate
7″ plate
5″ plate
Tea cups and saucers
Fruit
7″ baker (oval vegetable bowl)
Salt and pepper shakers
Covered casserole
Deep plate
7″ nappy
6″ Oatmeal
Tumblers (with handle)
Open Jug (also found with lid)
Tea Pot
Sauceboat
Creamer
Covered sugar

We have also found a 10″ dinner plate, 15″ platters, a covered syrup pitcher and two sizes of butter dishes . . . a half lb., and a quarter lb. There is also a juice set, (jug and tumblers), and recently a demmitasse cup and saucer has been discovered. These are all extremely hard to find.

Although it is uncertain just when Riviera was discontinued, it was sometime prior to 1950. Riviera is a challenge to collect; but you can be sure the effort will be worthwhile!

Top: 10″ dinner plates are very hard to come by! 9″ luncheon, 7″ bread and butter, shown in dark blue which is very unusual in this line (we have seen one other piece) and 6″ dessert bowl.

Tole Painters: All sizes make lovely·wall decorations!

Center: Two styles of platters, one with no handles, and one with closed handles. The light green one measures 11½″, the mauve blue one, 11¼″.

Bottom: Two more platters, 13¼″ and 12″. This is the other piece of cobalt blue that we know of. Notice that the wells in these two platters are square, and in the two above, the wells are oval.

The 13¼″ platter has also been found with an oval well, also a 15½″ one with an oval well.

Top: Tea pot, tea cups and saucers. We had a red cup that would have added a beautiful accent to the photo, but, alas, no saucer! Since then, we have received one as a gift from a thoughtful friend!

Bottom: In the top row, from left to right, you see a blue 5½″ fruit; a 9¼″ yellow baker with curving sides, and a soup plate, 8″.

In the lower left corner of the photo, there is a 9″ baker, with straight sides. The red nappy in the right corner measures 8¼″.

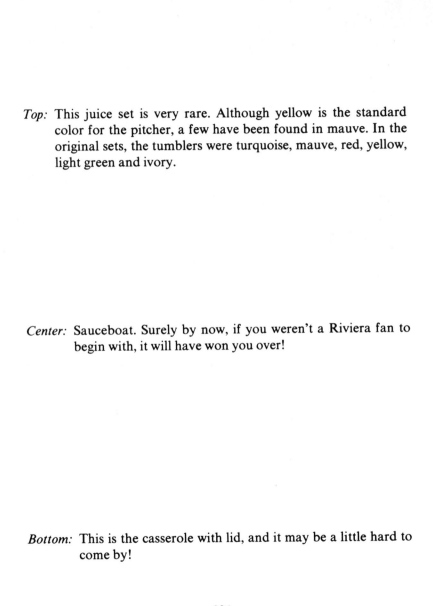

Top: This juice set is very rare. Although yellow is the standard color for the pitcher, a few have been found in mauve. In the original sets, the tumblers were turquoise, mauve, red, yellow, light green and ivory.

Center: Sauceboat. Surely by now, if you weren't a Riviera fan to begin with, it will have won you over!

Bottom: This is the casserole with lid, and it may be a little hard to come by!

Shown here is the covered jug, surrounded by four colors of the handled tumblers. The jugs are really quite hard to find, and have been found with cover in only light green and ivory. Below are the salt and pepper shakers. As you can see, there are six orange-like segments that make up the design . . . these were borrowed from the Tango line . . . yet they are compatible with the other Riviera pieces.

In the center of the picture are the two sizes of butter dishes. The large one holds a half lb., and they are much easier to find than the smaller quarter lb. size. The larger one is available in mauve, rose, yellow, spruce, light green, turquoise, maroon, dark blue, and red.

To the right are the regular creamer and sugar; above is the little covered syrup pitcher . . . a darling piece and rather rare.

Top: The batter set, complete with tray in cobalt, covered syrup pitcher and the tall covered jug — used for mixing, storing and pouring the batter for pancakes. These complete sets are quite unique, since they utilize one of the very rare cobalt blue pieces found in Riviera, and the cover for the tall jug — another hard to find item. In fact, the little covered syrup pitcher is also scarce.

Bottom: These tumblers are 4″ and 5¼″ tall and feature a band of Riviera Mauve. A collector has reported similar glassware styled with vertically paneled sides trimmed with one band of color — light green, mauve, yellow or red — at the rim. Bought at auction with a set of Riviera, the glassware was still in the original box marked "Juanita Beverage Set", Rosenthal and Ruben, Inc., Binghampton, N.Y., 1938. There are two each of the four colors in four different sizes of tumblers: 3″, 3½″, 4″ and 5¼″. Matching swizzle sticks complete the 48 piece set.

The demitasse cup and saucer is from the Century line, the forerunner of Riviera. Although only ivory has been reported, HLC indicates that they were produced in solid colors and sold with Riviera.

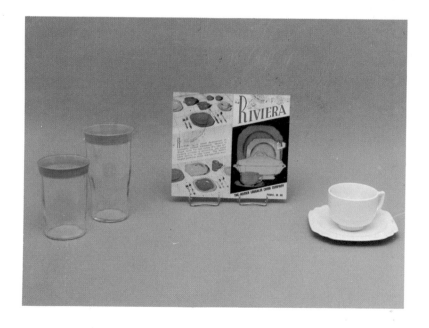

DECALED CENTURY

These are only a few examples of the many different decal decorations applied to Century shapes by Homer Laughlin. Many carry the particular name of the line on the back; and the year of manufacture is often represented by a two-digit number . . . 39, 42, etc. See page 80 for explanation of the dating code. Many collectors are fascinated by these decaled lines. We recently saw one heavily trimmed in gold, with a Colonial couple in formal attire, she curtsying and he lifting her hand. A friend tells of seeing a plate with a decal of Dick Tracy.

VIRGINIA ROSE

The butter dish bottom is decorated with one of the more popular Virginia Rose decals. To help us better understand this varied line, here is HLC's statement:

Virginia Rose is a shape name that incidentally was named for the daughter of our top management official at that time. This possibly has been our most popular line ever produced and was responsible for the construction of our plant #8, the world's largest single pottery at that time, basically to produce the Virginia Rose line. This plant began operations in 1929 and the shape was finally discontinued in the early 70's. Even now the same shape has been adopted by our hotel division and currently is one of the best selling shapes in the hotel and institutional field. There were many many decorations including decal with or without lines as well as patterns applied with air brushes through lead masks on the Virginia Rose shape. At that time all patterns were merely identified by number each preceded by the capital VR and a series of three numerals as the idea of applying a name to dinnerware decoration by manufacturers has merely been developed in recent years.

PRISCILLA PATTERN DINNERWARE

Only one of the many beautiful patterns of dinnerware fast becoming very collectable. As the photo indicates, this lovely line was offered with a wide assortment of serving pieces.

DOGWOOD

This lovely line of HLC dinnerware was produced in the early 1960's and is decorated with delicate sprigs of flowering dogwood.

SERENADE

Serenade was a pastel dinnerware line that was produced for only about three years in the early 40's. It was offered in four lovely pastel shades — yellow, green, pink and blue. Although not well accepted by the public when it was introduced, today's collectors find its soft delicate hues and dainty contours appealing. The pink bowl is a Kitchen Kraft casserole bottom, and is marked in the mold "Serenade". In addition to the pieces shown in the photo, these items were offered: deep plates, lug soups, pickles, platters, sauceboats and teapots.

JUBILEE

Jubilee was presented in 1948 by The Homer Laughlin China Company to celebrate their 75th year of ceramic leadership. The shape was simple, yet sophisticated, and the colors were Celedon Green, Shell Pink, Mist Grey and Cream Beige. The Jubilee calendar plate is dated 1953. The reverse side of the price list is reproduced below.

TANGO

Tango was a line introduced in the late 1930's . . . it was offered in blue, green, yellow and red. A price list dated 1937 indicates that it was sold through McLellan Stores Company, in New York City. In addition to the pieces shown in the photo, these were also listed: bakers, covered casseroles, creamers, covered sugars, dishes, fruits, nappies, and plates, 8" and 7".

RHYTHM

Rhythm was introduced at approximately the same time as the Harlequin line, and continued in production at least through the early 50's, perhaps even beyond. The color assortment listed on a 1952 price list reads: Harlequin yellow, chartreuse, grey, green, and burgandy . . . you may find others. In addition to those in the photo, stock items included nappies, 7"; fruits, 4"; plates, 4" and 7"; pickle dish; 8" dish; cream and covered sugar; sauceboat; teapot; casserole and cover (or nappy cover); and salt and pepper.

HOMER LAUGHLIN MEXICANA
. . . the Pattern that Started A Vogue

. . . so reads a trade paper from May, 1938 . . .

"When this Homer Laughlin pattern was first exhibited last July at the House Furnishing Show, it was an immediate smash hit. Its popularity has grown steadily ever since . . . and retailers have found it a constant and dependable source of profit. It started the vogue for the Mexican motif in crockery decoration which has since swept the country.

"And small wonder! For this Mexicana pattern is smart, colorful and attractive. It embodies the old-world atmosphere of Mexico with the modern verve and personality which is so appealing to American housewives. Applied to the pleasing, beautifully designed Homer Laughlin shapes, it presents a best seller of the first order."

The top photo shows this still-popular dinnerware. Notice that the bands of color on the inner rims are done in different colors . . . green, blue, and red. The Mexican motif tumblers are compatible with this design, and also were used to accessorize Fiesta.

The dinnerware at the bottom also has a Mexican flavor . . . this pattern is called Hacienda!

A third line of dinnerware produced by HLC with a "South-of-the-Border" flavor is called "Conchita", and was also introduced around 1938, evidenced by the dating code found on some of these pieces. (See page 80 for key to the dating code). Note the individual Kitchen Kraft casserole with matching decal. The popularity of this type of dinnerware must have been extraordinary . . . there was also a line of decaled Century called "Arizona", with a large green cactus, adobe house, yucca plant and pottery jug on an ivory glaze.

The tablecloth and napkins at the bottom are of the same vintage . . . the multicolored tumblers show both sides of one decorated with Spanish dancers, and the one in the center shows the Genuine Fiesta dancing girl — none are actually HLC related! On the right is the popular Mexicana pattern on a shape other than Century.

KITCHEN KRAFT AND
OVEN SERVE

From the very early 1930's Homer Laughlin China was the leading manufacturer of a very successful type of oven-to-table kitchen wares. These lines were called Oven-Serve and Kitchen Kraft. The variety of items offered and the many patterns and decaled lines that were made offer an endless field of interest for collectors today.

Top: Kitchen Kraft Mexicana. Shown are the 10" pie plate, 10" mixing bowl, spoon, fork, and pie server, 8½" casserole, and large salt and pepper shakers. Shown on the company's brochure in addition to these pieces are the small, medium, and large covered jars, the covered jug, and the 8" and 6" mixing bowls. You might find even others. This pattern, as well as Hacienda, is fast becoming very popular with collectors.

Bottom: Embossed line, Oven Serve. This is the line that carries the embossed floral pattern that decorates the handles of the Fiesta Kitchen Kraft spoon, fork and server. Shown on the top row, left to right: 7" round bowl, 8½" casserole, 6" mixing bowl with floral decal. *Bottom Row:* 8" oval baker, 9" plate with multicolor design underglaze, custard cup, and 5¾" turquoise fruit. You will occasionally find other colored glazes and various decal treatments on these shapes. This was quite an extensive line, and many unique pieces were produced. Watch for an almost identical line by T.S.&T.

Top: Large Kitchen Kraft mixing bowl; plate in the center is the Kitchen Kraft underplate — it measures 9" across, with a 1¼" rim. None of these have been found in Fiesta Kitchen Kraft colors, although they were shown on the original brochure.

The casserole on the right sits on a matching underplate.

Bottom: Aren't these ivory Kitchen Kraft items lovely decorated with delicate floral decals! The jug is rarely found with a cover in these decaled lines.

Top: These matching pieces must have been a housewife's delight. Here are the 10″ mixing bowl, 10″ pie plate and server . . . they're all marked Kitchen Kraft, Oven Serve.

Bottom: This is the Kitchen Kraft cake plate decorated with the Priscilla Pattern decal. The jug's delicate, full-blooming rose pattern is called Rhythm Rose. More often than not, these decaled jugs are not covered.

Top: We personally love the decaled pie plates. These are 10″ plates, in perfect condition and really quite beautiful!

Middle: This pattern is called Kitchen Bouquet . . . wouldn't it add a cheerful note to the kitchen! Shown are the 10″ pie plate, and the 13″ oval Kitchen Kraft platter. You may find these in the metal holders, too.

Bottom: Matching cake plate, 11″ deep dish pie plate, and server. Absolutely beautiful! These type pieces are not too easily found, rarely at a bargain.

THE AMERICAN POTTER

As a tribute to the American Potter, six pottery companies united their efforts and jointly built and operated an actual working kiln at the 1939-40 World's Fair in New York. A variety of plates, vases, figural items and bowls in a myriad of colors were produced — these were marked with an ink stamp "The American Potter, 1939 (or 40), World's Fair Exhibit, Joint Exhibit of Capitol and Labor."

The Homer Laughlin China Company entry — proudly designed by Rhead — is shown in the top photo. In the center of each plate, you can see the Trylon and the Parisphere, adopted symbols of the Fair.

In the bottom photo are the entries from the other five companies. The cake set is from The Cronin China Co., Minerva O, National Brotherhood of Operative Potters. The 10" bowl in the center is marked Paden City Pottery, Made In USA, and the 10¾" plate on the right is marked Knowles, Joint Exhibit of Capitol and Labor. The smaller piece is actually the bottom half of a marmalade, and is embossed with the Trylon and Parisphere and the words "New York World's Fair". It's 3" tall and is marked "Edwin M. Knowles, China Co., Semi Vitreous".

Although not mentioned on the original pamphlet with the other companies and their entries, the pitcher is a World's Fair souvenir marked Porcelier Trade Mark, Vitreous Hand Decorated China, Made in U.S.A.

Top: The Potters' Plates are possibly the easiest of the World's Fair items to find. There were two — on the left. The Potter at His Wheel; and the companion plate on the right — The Artist Decorating the Vase. Turquoise and Light Green have also been found. Of course, to find one in the original box would be most unusual. Also shown is a cup and saucer embossed with signs of the Zodiac . . . another rarity!

Bottom: This is a beautiful display of hand turned vases — especially the small ones are becoming very popular. They are from 1½" to 2¾" high and all are marked with the ink stamp. The larger vases are from 5" to 7" tall; the cobalt blue piece on the far right is a candleholder. Note the red individual creamer from the Harlequin line, "World's Fair" etched on the side.

Top: Two figural pitchers, each 5″ tall. Martha Washington is marked The American Potter, New York World's Fair, with the year 1940 on a raised disk superimposed over a Trylon. George Washington is marked First Edition For Collectors, Limited to 100 Pieces, The American Potter, New York's World Fair, 1939. It is numbered 37. The tall vase measures 7″ and is marked with the ink stamp.

On the second row, the Martha and George Washington pitchers are each 2″ tall and are marked. These are sometimes found in bisque, and one pair in mauve blue has been reported.

The toothpick holder in the center is 2″ high; the salt and pepper shakers are 2½″ . . . neither are marked.

Bottom: The four season plates are 4¼″ across:
Spring shows a man fishing for trout;
Summer depicts a family picnicking;
Autumn shows a man hunting with his dog;
and Winter, a couple skating.

In the early 1900's, evidently attempting to enter the art pottery field, the Homer Laughlin China Company produced a unique line of art china. It was marked in gold with the eagle and the line name, Laughlin Art China. Examples of this ware are very rare. They are characteristically very colorful and are usually gold trimmed.

And so there seems to be no end to this area of collecting fun! At first we were strictly "Fiesta collectors", who soon discovered Harlequin . . . and Riviera . . . Amberstone . . . World's Fair . . . Kitchen Kraft . . . decaled dinnerware lines . . . "go-alongs", the metal, wooden, glass accessories . . . advertising pieces . . .

When we finished the second edition, we were sure the "Story of Fiesta" was at last complete — and now here we are concluding the third! We find ourselves slightly dazed and very pleased to have been able to add sufficient new "bait" to keep you "fishin' " for a few more years, thanks to all of you who contributed your discoveries. A unique coffee server belongs to a lucky collector who thoughtfully sent us a photo might have been the work of an imaginative employee on his coffee break . . . or it may have been done outside the plant. Its interior is ivory, while the outside glaze is a mottled green and gold!

Considering the discoveries that have been made these past few months — the HLC child's set, unusual colors, even new pieces never before listed — who knows! Those beautiful footed Fiesta mugs may not be just a dream! Maybe . . . just maybe . . . that same fellow who dreamed up that Harlequin lamp, or that motley glazed coffee server, made some mugs for us!

Gone Fishin' . . .

SUGGESTED VALUES

Values are suggested for items that are in mint condition . . . that is to say, no chips, "chigger bites", or "dings"! Bad glazing and scratches would also reduce the value. The three sager pin marks that are evident on the underside of many pieces are characteristic, and result from the technique employed during the firing process. These should have no adverse effect.

We have attempted to locate both a high and a low range that would allow for the differences in demand in various parts of the country. In a nationwide sampling of dealers we found that while prices in the East are very high, in some parts of Michigan and Wisconsin, they have not risen to a great extent over last year. Through the Midwest prices seem to be average to high average, and items that are very popular and rather high in one area, are not bringing these prices in another.

The 50's colors are highly prized and are harder to find, and in most cases have become as desirable as red. For these colors: grey, rose, chartreuse, dark green (and med. green) . . . and of course, any *red* piece, Harlequin and Riviera included, add 25% to the *high* side of the range. Some items may be rarely found in a common color, when possible we will indicate a price for a piece such as this in the listing . . . otherwise, the high side would apply.

Actual measurements may vary as much as ¾″ from those listed in the price guide. For instance, the factory lists a dinner plate as 10″, when it actually measures 10½″. In those instances where actual measurements vary more than ½″ from factory sizes we will show actual size in parenthesis.

Color code:
    * made in six original colors; red, dark blue, old ivory, yellow, light green, and turquoise.
    ** made in eleven colors — six original plus rose, grey, chartreuse, dark green, and medium green.
    *** made in ten colors, no med. green

SUGGESTED VALUES FOR FIESTA

Page 39
Top Row:
    (14⅜") 15" Chop plate*** 6.00-   9.00
    (12¼") 13" Chop plate** 4.00-   6.00
Middle:
    11⅝" Compartment plate* (no turquoise)   7.00- 10.00
    10½" Compartment plate*** 5.00-   7.00
Bottom:
    (10½") 10" Dinner plate** 4.00-   5.00
    (9½") 9" Luncheon** 2.00-   3.00
    (7⅜") 7" Bread and butter** 1.50-   2.50
    (6⅜") 6" Dessert plate** 1.00-   2.00
Page 41
    8" Deep plate** 5.00-   7.00
    Cream soup cup** 5.00-   8.00
        (in med. green) 12.00- 16.00
    7⅝" Individual salad bowl 10.00- 14.00
      (med. green, red more common than turquoise and yellow)
    6" Dessert bowl** 4.00-   6.00
        (in med. green) 15.00- 20.00
    4¾" Fruit** 3.50-   4.50
        (in med. green) 15.00- 20.00
    5½" Fruit** 4.00-   5.00
Page 43
Top:
    Coffee pot, regular*** 20.00- 25.00
    Tea cups** 5.00-   7.00
    Saucers** 75-   1.50
Middle:
    Egg cups*** 10.00- 12.00
Lower Right:
    Tom & Jerry mugs** 10.00- 13.00
        (in red) 25.00- 30.00

Page 45

Top:

Disk water pitcher, 2 qt.**	7.00-	12.00
10 oz. Tumbler*	8.00-	11.00

Bottom:

Covered sugar**	4.00-	6.00
Creamer, reg.**	3.00-	4.00
Creamer, stick handle*	4.00-	6.00
Utility tray*	5.00-	7.00
Salt and Peppers**	3.00-	5.00

Page 47

Top:

Oval platter, 12"**	4.00-	8.00
9½" Nappy*	6.00-	8.00
8½" Nappy**	5.00-	6.00
9½" Salad bowl in yellow	12.00-	18.00

Center, Left:

Footed salad bowl*	40.00-	55.00

Bottom, Right:

Fruit bowl, 11¾"*	30.00-	40.00

Page 49

Top:

11" Nested bowl, #7*	20.00-	30.00
10" Nested bowl, #6*	15.00-	20.00
9" Nested bowl, #5*	12.00-	14.00
8" Nested bowl, #4*	10.00-	12.00
7" Nested bowl, #3*	8.00-	10.00
6" Nested bowl, #2*	8.00-	10.00
5" Nested bowl, #1*	10.00-	15.00
Any size lid	20.00-	30.00

Center, Left:

Gravy boat**	6.00-	10.00

Bottom, Right:

Casserole**	18.00-	22.00
(in med. green)	30.00-	35.00

Page 51

Top:

Relish tray*	22.00-	30.00

Comport, 12"* 16.00- 18.00
Bottom:
Coffee Pot, After Dinner* 35.00- 50.00
Coffee cups, A.D.*** 9.00- 12.00
Saucers, A.D.*** 2.00- 4.00
    (red, cup and saucer) 16.00- 20.00
    (50's colors, cup and saucer) 30.00- 35.00
Page 53
Top:
Carafe, 3 pt.* 20.00- 27.00
Ice pitcher, 2 qt.* 12.00- 16.00
Bottom:
2 pt. jug.*** 8.00- 14.00
Covered onion soup* 50.00- 60.00
    (in turquoise)................. 85.00-100.00
    (in red) 70.00- 75.00
Page 55
Top:
Ash tray** 7.00- 10.00
Sweets comport* 8.00- 12.00
Mustard* 27.00- 35.00
Marmalade* 40.00- 45.00
Syrup pitcher* 40.00- 50.00
Bottom:
Tea pot, large* 18.00- 24.00
Tea pot, med.** 12.00- 16.00
Page 57
Top:
Vase, 12"* 65.00- 75.00
Vase, 10"* 60.00- 75.00
Vase, 8"* 35.00- 45.00
Bud vase* 10.00- 14.00
Bottom:
Candleholder, tripod, pr.* 40.00- 55.00
Candleholder, bulb, pr.* 12.00- 16.00
Page 59
Top:
Handled chop plate, 13"* 25.00- 30.00

French casserole (Yellow)	40.00- 50.00
Individual sugar, creamer, tray,	
in yellow and navy blue	35.00- 40.00
Bottom:	
Juice pitcher, 30 oz., yellow	4.00- 6.00
(in red)	20.00- 30.00
Juice tumbler, 5 oz.	
(original six colors and rose)	5.00- 7.00
(in chartreuse)	20.00- 25.00

Page 61

Metal holders only:	
for salt, pepper, mustard	25.00- 30.00
for Kitchen Kraft casserole	7.00- 10.00
for marmalade	12.00- 18.00
Fiestawood bowl.	30.00- 40.00
3 tier tidbit tray	20.00- 25.00
Serenade juice set,	
30 oz. pitcher	17.00- 25.00
5 oz. tumbler	18.00- 20.00

Page 63

Metal holders only:	
for 9½" nappy	6.00- 8.00
for cream soup, jam set	20.00- 25.00
for juice set	12.00- 17.00
Tea pot, with metal dripolator insert,	
complete unit	35.00- 45.00
Sta-brite stainless flatware with colored plastic handles	
3 pc. place setting	4.00- 6.00
Fiestawood Lazy Suzan, 20"	30.00- 40.00

Page 65

Top:	
Tom & Jerry bowl.	40.00- 55.00
Tom & Jerry mugs	18.00- 20.00
Middle:	
Advertising mugs, ea.	14.00- 17.00
(blanks)	10.00- 12.00
Bottom:	
7" plate	1.00- 2.00

9″ plate	1.00- 2.00
10″ plate	1.00- 2.00

Page 67
Top:

Tall mug, hotel china	7.00- 10.00
Sit 'n Sip carton only	5.00- 7.00
Tall mug, with advertising	9.00- 12.00
Nursery mug	15.00- 20.00
Sit 'n Sip sets	18.00- 22.00
Advertising mug in Fiesta color	15.00- 20.00

Bottom:

Advertising mug, color inside	14.00- 17.00
Mug with Antique Car decal	18.00- 25.00
Mug with color inside, blank	12.00- 14.00

Page 69
Top:

15″ Chop plate with decal	25.00- 32.00
Tom & Jerry mug	3.00- 4.00
Tom & Jerry bowl.................	10.00- 12.00

Bottom:

Fiestawood tray, 16½″	20.00- 30.00
Advertising ash tray	25.00- 30.00
Metal base only...................	15.00- 20.00
Wooden handle only	5.00- 7.50

Page 71
Top:

5″ Fruit (Lazarus).................	10.00- 15.00
Egg cup (Lazarus).................	20.00- 25.00

Middle:

15″ Chop plate with floral decal	25.00- 35.00
7″ Plate with floral decal	5.00- 10.00
13″ Chop plate with turkey decal	35.00- 50.00

Bottom:

Calendar plate, 1954, 10″............	12.00- 15.00
"Good Luck", 1955, 9″	22.00- 30.00
Calendar plate, 1955, 10″............	16.00- 18.00

Page 73

Top:

Plate with floral decal, 10″	8.00-	10.00
Tea cup with floral decal	7.00-	10.00
Saucer with floral decal	4.00-	6.00
Fruit with floral decal, 4¾″	4.00-	6.00

Bottom, Left:

Footed salad bowl with decal	50.00-	65.00

Bottom, Right:

Cake plate, 10″	30.00-	40.00

Page 75

Top Row:

Creamer, experimental, 4″	16.00-	24.00
Comport, 10″ × 2½″, rare	65.00-	90.00
Individual tea pot, with cover, experimental	75.00-	100.00
Individual red creamer	22.00-	30.00
(in turquoise)	40.00-	50.00
Individual turquoise tray	35.00-	50.00
Medium Green fruit, 4¾″	15.00-	20.00
Relish section, experimental	30.00-	40.00
Original Fiesta carton	8.00-	10.00

Page 77

Top:

Saturday Evening Post, intact	15.00-	20.00
Fiesta price listing, 1965	3.00-	5.00
Fiesta price listing, 1939	7.00-	10.00
Menu, any size	5.00-	7.00
Sheet of decals	15.00-	25.00
Corn package	5.00-	7.00

Bottom:

Canister set	20.00-	27.00
Napkin Holder	12.00-	18.00

Page 79

Top:

Hankscraft egg cooker, complete set		
(with egg cups and tray)	40.00-	45.00
(cooker only)	30.00-	40.00

(egg cups, as shown)	3.00- 4.00

Bottom:

Footed cake stand	30.00- 35.00

Page 81

Top:

Nested bowl set, 5″, 6″, 7″, 8″, 9½″ . . .	20.00- 25.00

Bottom:

HLC Child's set

Mug	20.00- 25.00
Bowl, 5¼″	20.00- 25.00
Plate, 7″	15.00- 20.00

FIESTA CASUALS

Values apply to both patterns.

Page 83

12½″ Oval platter	15.00- 20.00
10″ Plate	5.00- 8.00
7″ Plate	4.00- 6.00
Saucer	4.00- 6.00

AMBERSTONE

Page 85

Dinner plate	3.50
Dessert dish	1.50
Bread and Butter	1.50
Coffee cup with saucer	4.00- 5.00
Vegetable bowl	4.50
Covered sugar	4.00
Creamer	3.00
Oval platter	6.00
Large soup plate	4.00
Ash tray	10.00- 14.00
Salt and pepper, pr.	6.00- 9.00
Salad plate	1.50
Soup cereal	2.00
Covered casserole	15.00
Sauce boat	8.00- 10.00
Relish tray	10.00
Coffee server	15.00- 20.00
Tea server	12.00

Covered butter	24.00	
Round serving platter..............	12.00	
Jumbo salad bowl	6.00-	7.00
Covered jam jar	22.00	
Serving pitcher, disk	12.00-	18.00
Jumbo mug	4.00	
Pie plate	20.00	

CASUALSTONE

Items in plain Antique Gold are priced with Ironstone, since they are interchangeable.

Page 87

Oval platter/gold design	8.00-	10.00
10" Plate/gold design	3.00-	4.00
Saucer/gold design	1.00-	2.00

FIESTA IRONSTONE

Prices apply to Antique Gold, Turf Green, and all restyled items in red.

Page 89

Med. tea pot	5.00-	8.00
13" Oval platter..................	2.00-	4.00
Coffee server	8.00-	10.00
10" Dinner plate	2.00-	2.50
Disk water pitcher	5.00-	7.00
Sugar/cover.....................	2.00-	2.50
Creamer	1.50-	2.00
Marmalade	12.00-	15.00
Large nappy	3.00-	4.00
Small fruit	1.50-	2.50
Salad bowl	5.00-	7.00
Tea cups........................	2.00-	2.50
Saucer	.50-	.75
Sauceboat	2.50-	4.00
Sauceboat stand	5.00-	8.00
(in red)	20.00	
7" Plate	.85-	1.00
Coffee mug	3.00-	4.00
Covered casserole	6.00-	8.00
Shakers, pr.	2.00-	2.50

Ash tray 2.50-   4.00

FIESTA KITCHEN KRAFT

Page 93
Covered refrigerator jars, mixed colors   30.00- 37.50
Covered jug, either size 50.00- 65.00

Page 95
Top:
Casserole, 8½" 24.00- 30.00
Casserole, 7½" 24.00- 30.00
Individual casserole 25.00- 35.00

Middle:
Large covered jar 45.00- 55.00
Med. covered jar 40.00- 55.00
Small covered jar 40.00- 55.00

Bottom:
10" mixing bowl 20.00- 25.00
8" mixing bowl 15.00- 20.00
6" mixing bowl 10.00- 15.00

Page 97
Top:
Cake plate 13.00- 18.00
Pie plate, 10" 16.00- 20.00
Pie Plate, 9" 15.00- 18.00

Middle:
Metal holders only:
for 10" pie plate 6.00- 12.00
for casserole 6.00- 10.00
for platter 10.00- 15.00
Oval platter, only, 13" 30.00- 40.00

Bottom:
Spoon 20.00- 24.00
Fork 22.00- 25.00
Server 22.00- 30.00
Salt and peppers 20.00- 30.00

HARLEQUIN

Page 103
Top:
10" Plate 1.50-   2.00

9" Plate	1.00-	1.50
7" Plate	.85-	1.00
6" Plate	.50-	.75

Center:

13" Platter	3.00-	5.00
11" Platter	2.00-	4.00

Bottom:

Deep plate	2.00-	3.00
36's Oatmeal, 6½"	1.50-	2.00
5½" Fruit	1.00-	1.50
Cream soup	2.50-	3.50

Page 105

9" Nappy	2.50-	3.50
36's Bowl	3.00-	4.00
Casserole with lid	12.00-	18.00
9" Oval baker	2.50-	3.50
Individual salad bowl, 7"	3.00-	4.00

Page 107

Top:

Service water jug	8.00-	10.00
Water tumblers	4.50-	6.00

Bottom:

Tea pot	8.00-	12.00
Tea cups	2.00-	3.00
Saucer	.50-	.75

Page 109

Top:

Covered sugar	2.50-	3.00
Creamer, regular	2.00-	2.50
Creamer with high lip	14.00-	17.00
Salt and peppers	2.00-	3.00
Marmalade	20.00-	30.00
Novelty creamer	3.00-	5.00

Bottom:

Sauceboat	2.50-	4.00
Tumbler with car decal	8.00-	12.00
22 oz. Jug	5.00-	8.00
(in grey, chartreuse, dk. gr., med. gr.)	10.00-	15.00

Page 111
Top:

Saucer/ash tray	14.00- 16.00
Nut dish, 3″	3.00- 4.00
Syrup	35.00- 45.00
Large cup, tankard	20.00- 25.00
Ash tray, reg.	12.00- 14.00
Ash tray, basketweave	15.00- 20.00
Covered butter	22.00- 25.00
Perfume bottle	15.00- 20.00

Bottom:

5 pc. Relish tray	20.00- 25.00
Nut dish	12.00- 17.00

Page 113
Top:

Candleholders, pr.	25.00- 30.00
Double egg cup	3.00- 4.00
Individual egg cup	5.00- 8.00
Coffee cup, After Dinner	4.00- 5.00
(in 50's colors)	8.00- 10.00
Saucer, A.D.	2.00- 2.50
(in 50's colors)	3.00- 4.00

Bottom:

Spoon rest, in Harlequin colors	70.00- 80.00
(in 50's colors and red)	100.00-125.00
(with original label)	110.00-125.00
(in 50's colors, with label)	140.00-175.00
Advertising spoon rest	50.00- 65.00
(white, no lettering)	40.00- 50.00

Page 115
Top:

Metal holder and tumbler	7.50- 10.00
Donkey with salt and peppers	5.00- 10.00
Individual creamer	4.00- 6.00

Bottom:

Large tankard with saucer, set	27.50- 35.00
Lamp base	50.00- 75.00
Harlequin pamphlet	7.00- 12.00

Page 117
Top:

Harlequin animals	30.00-	40.00

Bottom:

Mavericks	15.00-	25.00

Page 121
Top:

10″ Plate	2.50-	4.00
9″ Plate	2.00-	3.00
7″ Plate	1.00-	1.50
6″ Plate	.75-	1.00

Center:

11½″ Platter, oval well	3.00-	4.00
11¼″ Platter, with handles	3.00-	4.00

Bottom:

13″ Platter with handles	4.00-	6.00
12″ Platter with handles	4.00-	6.00

Page 123
Top:

Tea pot	12.00-	16.00
Tea cup	3.00-	4.00
Saucer	1.00-	1.50

Bottom:

5½″ Fruit	1.00-	1.50
9¼″ Oval baker	2.00-	4.00
Deep plate	2.00-	4.00
9″ Oval baker	2.00-	4.00
8¼″ Nappy	3.00-	4.50

Page 125
Top:

Juice jug, yellow	20.00-	25.00
(in mauve)	35.00-	45.00
Juice tumbler	10.00-	12.00

Center, Left:

Sauceboat	2.50-	4.00

Bottom, Right:

Casserole with lid	12.00-	18.00

Page 127
Handled tumblers 10.00- 12.00
Covered jug 14.00- 20.00
Quarter lb. butter, cover 20.00- 24.00
Covered syrup 18.00- 24.00
Salt and peppers 3.00- 4.00
One half lb. butter, cover 22.00- 25.00
Creamer, reg. 2.00- 3.00
Covered sugar 3.00- 4.00
Page 129
Top:
Complete batter set 45.00- 55.00
Bottom:
Tumblers 2.50- 4.00
Riviera pamphlet 7.00- 12.00
Demitasse cup and saucer 7.50- 10.00

DECALED CENTURY

Page 131
Top:
9″ Plate, Old English scene 1.50- 2.50
9″ Plate, Columbine 1.50- 2.50
9″ Plate, Wild Rose 1.50- 2.50
Center:
13″ Platter, gold decal 1.50- 3.00
11″ Platter, floral needlepoint 1.50- 3.00
Bottom:
Sugar, cottage and garden scene 2.00- 3.00
Creamer 2.00- 3.00
Virginia Rose butter with cover 20.00- 25.00

PRISCILLA PATTERN

Page 133
Coffee pot 12.00- 20.00
Fruit bowl, 9½″ 7.00- 10.00
Sugar 4.00- 5.00
Creamer 3.00- 4.00
Gravy boat 4.00- 6.00
Cup and saucer 3.50- 4.50

Oval vegetable, 9″	3.00-	4.00
Soup, 8½″	3.50-	4.00
Platter, 13½″	4.00-	6.00
Dinner plate, 9″	3.00-	4.00
Luncheon plate, 8″	2.00-	3.00
Dessert plate, 6″	1.50-	2.00
Fruit, 5″	1.50-	2.50

DOGWOOD

Page 133

Plate, 9″	2.00-	3.00
Fruit, 5½″	2.00-	2.50
Dessert plate, 6½″	1.50-	2.00

SERENADE

Page 135

Chop plate, 13″	4.00-	6.00
Dinner plate, 9″	2.50-	3.50
Bread and butter plate, 7″	1.50-	2.00
Cup and saucer	3.50-	4.50
Fruit, 6″	2.00-	2.50
Shakers, pr.	5.00-	6.00
Vegetable bowl, 9″	3.00-	4.00
Casserole, with lid	7.00-	10.00
Serenade Kitchen Kraft casserole with lid	7.00-	10.00

JUBILEE

Page 135

Plate 10″, calendar	3.00-	6.00
Jubilee pamphlet	5.00-	10.00

TANGO

Page 137

Egg cups	3.00-	4.00
Cup and saucer	3.00-	4.00
Dessert plate, 6″	1.00-	1.50
Shakers, pr.	1.50-	3.00
Deep soup	1.50-	2.50

RHYTHM

Page 137

Plate, 9″	2.00-	3.00
Cup and saucer	3.00-	4.00
Dessert plate, 6″	1.00-	2.00
Fruit, 5½″	1.00-	2.00

MEXICANA

Page 139

Top:

36's Oatmeal, 6″	2.50-	3.00
Fruit, 5¼″	1.50-	2.00
Glass tumblers, ea.	4.00-	6.00
Tea cup	4.00-	5.00
Saucer	.75-	1.00
Deep plate	3.00-	4.00
Plate, 9″	1.50-	2.50

HACIENDA

Page 139

Bottom:

5½″ Fruit	1.50-	2.00
36's Oatmeal	2.00-	2.50
Creamer	2.00-	3.00
Covered sugar	3.00-	4.00
Plate, 7″	.75-	1.25
Plate, 9″	1.50-	2.50

CONCHITA

Page 141

Platter	7.00-	10.00
Plate	3.50-	5.00
Cup and saucer	4.00-	6.00
Fruit	3.00-	4.00
Sugar	4.50-	6.00
Creamer	3.00-	4.00
Kitchen Kraft casserole	20.00-	25.00

Bottom:

Tablecloth and napkins	22.00-	27.00
Tumblers, either style	2.50-	4.00
Cup and saucer	4.00-	6.00

KITCHEN KRAFT MEXICANA

Page 143

Top:

10" Pie plate	12.00-	15.00
10" Mixing bowl	12.00-	17.00
Spoon	16.00-	20.00
Fork	16.00-	20.00
Server	16.00-	20.00
8" Casserole	16.00-	20.00
Salt and Pepper, pr.	18.00-	24.00

EMBOSSED LINE, OVEN SERVE

Page 143

Bottom:

7" Nappy	1.50-	2.00
8½" Casserole	4.00-	6.00
6" Mixing bowl	1.50-	2.00
8" Oval baker	1.50-	2.00
9" Plate	1.00-	1.50
Custard cup	1.00-	1.50
Fruit, 5¾"	1.00-	1.50

Page 145

Top:

Kitchen Kraft bowl with decal	7.50-	10.00
Underplate, 9"	6.00-	10.00
Casserole	5.00-	7.00

Bottom:

Covered jar, sm., med. or large	20.00-	25.00
Stack set unit, ea.	5.00-	7.00
(lid)	6.00-	8.00
Covered jug	15.00-	20.00
Individual casserole	15.00-	20.00

Page 147

Top:

10" Mixing bowl	4.00-	6.00
Server	6.00-	8.00
Pie plate, 10"	5.00-	7.50

Bottom:

Cake plate	5.00-	7.50

```
Jug, open . . . . . . . . . . . . . . . . . . . . . . . .          6.00-  8.00
      (with lid)  . . . . . . . . . . . . . . . . . . . .        15.00- 20.00
Page 149
Top:
   10" Pie plate/tulips . . . . . . . . . . . . . . . .          5.00-  7.50
   10" Pie plate/wild rose . . . . . . . . . . . . .            5.00-  7.50
   10" Pie plate/floral . . . . . . . . . . . . . . . .         5.00-  7.50
Middle:
   10" Pie plate/Kitchen Bouquet . . . . . . .                  5.00-  7.50
   13" Platter/Kitchen Bouquet . . . . . . . .                  5.00-  7.50
Bottom:
   Cake plate/floral  . . . . . . . . . . . . . . . . .         5.00-  7.50
   11" Pie plate . . . . . . . . . . . . . . . . . . . . .      6.00-  8.00
   Server . . . . . . . . . . . . . . . . . . . . . . . . . .   6.00-  8.00
```

THE AMERICAN POTTER

```
Page 151
Top:
   HLC World's Fair plate, '39 or '40 . . . .                  25.00- 30.00
Bottom:
   Cake set . . . . . . . . . . . . . . . . . . . . . . . .    17.00- 22.00
   Bowl . . . . . . . . . . . . . . . . . . . . . . . . . . .  15.00- 22.00
   Plate . . . . . . . . . . . . . . . . . . . . . . . . . .   18.00- 22.00
   Marmalade and cover  . . . . . . . . . . . . . .           12.00- 16.00
   Pitcher . . . . . . . . . . . . . . . . . . . . . . . . .   15.00- 20.00
Page 153
Top:
   Potter's Plate . . . . . . . . . . . . . . . . . . . . .    10.00- 16.00
   Original box  . . . . . . . . . . . . . . . . . . . . .     10.00- 15.00
   Zodiac cup and saucer . . . . . . . . . . . . . .          25.00- 35.00
Bottom:
   Green vase, 5½" . . . . . . . . . . . . . . . . . .         15.00- 18.00
   Turquoise vase, 7"  . . . . . . . . . . . . . . . .         18.00- 24.00
   Yellow, 4½" . . . . . . . . . . . . . . . . . . . . . .     15.00- 18.00
   Small vase, any size  . . . . . . . . . . . . . . .         12.00- 15.00
   Bowl . . . . . . . . . . . . . . . . . . . . . . . . . . .   8.00- 12.00
   Candleholder, 2" . . . . . . . . . . . . . . . . . .        15.00- 20.00
   Individual creamer . . . . . . . . . . . . . . . .         15.00- 20.00
```

Page 155

Top:

5″ Martha Washington pitcher	22.00- 24.00
5″ George Washington pitcher	14.00- 18.00
7″ Vase	12.00- 15.00
2″ Martha Washington pitcher	14.00- 16.00
2″ George Washington pitcher	14.00- 16.00
(in bisque)	7.00- 10.00
(in mauve)	25.00- 35.00
Toothpick holder	16.00- 18.00
Salt and peppers, pr.	14.00- 18.00

Bottom:

Four seasons bowls, ea.	15.00- 20.00

INDEX